USE-VALUE
ASSESSMENT

OF RURAL LAND
IN THE UNITED STATES

USE-VALUE ASSESSMENT

OF RURAL LAND

IN THE UNITED STATES

JOHN E. ANDERSON and
RICHARD W. ENGLAND

LINCOLN INSTITUTE
OF LAND POLICY
CAMBRIDGE, MASSACHUSETTS

Library of Congress Cataloging-in-Publication Data

Anderson, John E. (John Edwin), 1951–
    Use-value assessment of rural land in the United States / John E. Anderson and Richard W. England.
        pages cm
    Includes index.
    Summary: "Explains the origins, key features, and implementation of use-value assessment (UVA) programs in property taxation in the United States during the last half-century. Intended audience consists of academics who study public finance, agricultural and land economics, urban economics and regional planning, and environmental economics; and state tax and conservation. Covers theory, practice, criticism, and reform recommendations"—Provided by publisher.
    ISBN 978-1-55844-297-9 (alk. paper)
    1. Property tax—United States.   2. Tax assessment—United States.   3. Land value taxation—United States.   I. England, Richard W.   II. Title.
    HJ4120.U55A53 2014
    336.22'5—dc23   2014009415

Designed by Westchester Publishing Services.

Composed in Minion Pro by Westchester Publishing Services in Danbury, Connecticut.
Printed and bound by Puritan Press Inc., in Hollis, New Hampshire.
The paper is Rolland Enviro100, an acid-free, 100 percent PCW recycled sheet.

MANUFACTURED IN THE UNITED STATES OF AMERICA

Contents

USE-VALUE
ASSESSMENT
OF RURAL LAND
IN THE UNITED STATES

1 \ Introduction to Use-Value Assessment

A short drive north of Boston, the town of Bedford sits to the immediate southwest of New Hampshire's largest city, Manchester. Bedford was incorporated in 1750, during the colonial era, and named after the fourth Duke of Bedford. It is now an affluent and growing community with a population exceeding 21,000 and a median family income greater than $127,000 in 2010. As recently as 1970, the U.S. Census counted fewer than 5,900 residents in what was then a fairly rural New England town.

Bedford has grown in population during recent decades, and much of its rural landscape has been developed for a variety of reasons. Jobs, hospitals, and a regional airport are available in nearby Manchester, for example. Commuters to suburban and downtown Boston have immediate access to the region's interstate highways and turnpikes. Three of Bedford's public elementary schools were among the state's top 10 for combined math and reading scores in 2011–2012. The town's 2011 property tax rate, adjusted to full market value, was in the lower half of the distribution for all communities in New Hampshire.

Attributes such as these have attracted homebuilders and affluent households to Bedford for a number of decades. If you were to search today for undeveloped land on which to build a new subdivision, however, you would make a startling discovery. Although vacant parcels are still available, their assessments for tax purposes vary tremendously from property to property. One large tract that is zoned residential and located near the Everett Turnpike with frontage on a local street is assessed at $7,865 per acre. Another sizable parcel close to the turnpike with frontage on a cul-de-sac is assessed at $10,047 per acre. In the very same neighborhood, however, is an even larger tract of vacant land that the town assessor values at a mere $127 per acre for tax purposes. Looking more closely at the landscape in Bedford, one finds nearly 200 undeveloped parcels covering more than 13 percent of the town's land area that are assessed far below market value—at an average of $155 per acre.

How can there be such dramatic differences in the assessment of land values within the same community and even within the same neighborhood? Has the town assessor failed to treat property owners fairly and equally, as required by state law? Are the variations in price due exclusively to zoning restrictions or location factors? Not at all. Nearly all states across the country permit and even require local assessors to value some parcels of undeveloped land far below their fair market values for the purpose of levying local property taxes. This practice, often called *use-value assessment* (UVA), is perfectly legal and represents a major policy shift in local taxation during the last 50 years or more.

Use-value assessment deserves to be closely inspected and carefully analyzed because taxation of real property has always been and still remains a key pillar of our federal political system. In 2011, for example, the general revenues of state governments and local governments in the United States totaled $2,265 billion and $1,689 billion, respectively. During recent decades, local governments have come to depend on federal and state governments for intergovernmental transfers or grants, which total $554 billion in 2011. However, local jurisdictions still have to raise a lot of funds through their own tax systems to pay for public schools, police and fire protection, and other local services. During 2011, tax revenues of municipalities, counties, and school districts equaled $578 billion. Of this total, $429 billion came from local property taxation. (State governments raised another $14 billion in that year by taxing real property.) During recent times, property taxes have been the source of roughly a third of state and local government tax revenue in the United States (Barnett and Vidal 2013). Elected officials and citizens cannot afford to ignore the continued importance of the property tax in this country and the significant modification of that tax represented by use-value assessment of undeveloped land.

As discussed in greater detail in chapter 2, UVA programs have been adopted across the nation in part because of concerns about the loss of

FIGURE 1.1
Developed Land, 1982–2007

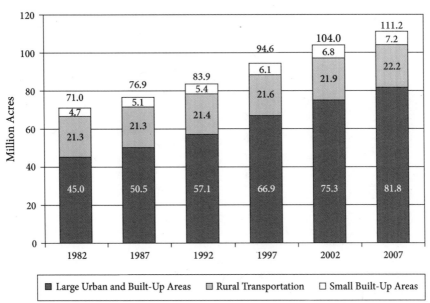

SOURCE: Natural Resources Conservation Service, *2007 National Resources Inventory*, 7.

farm, ranch, and forest land resulting from long-term growth of metro-politan regions. From Atlanta to Kansas City to Seattle, cities and their suburbs have displaced more than 40 million acres of rural land during recent decades, as shown in figure 1.1. During the quarter century after 1982, the developed areas of Arizona, Florida, and Georgia roughly dou-bled. Texas had already developed more than five million acres by 1982 but increased that area by more than two-thirds by 2007. Even slowly growing states such as Illinois, Massachusetts, and New York developed substantial amounts of rural land during the same period, as shown in table 1.1. From 1982 to 2007, the developed area of the entire United States grew from 3.76 percent of its total land area to 5.89 percent, an increase of more than two percentage points.

This continuing urbanization of the American landscape has prompted state and local governments to adopt a number of public policies that aim

TABLE 1.1

Growth of Developed Land Area in Selected States, 1982–2007

	Developed Area in 1982 (Millions of Acres)	Percent Change in Developed Area, 1982–2007
Arizona	1.02	97.1
California	4.08	51.2
Florida	2.77	99.0
Georgia	2.23	108.3
Illinois	2.62	29.0
Massachusetts	1.09	58.0
New York	2.81	35.1
Texas	5.07	67.9

SOURCE: Natural Resources Conservation Service, *2007 National Resources Inventory*, table 1.

to regulate the conversion of rural land to developed uses. These policies include agricultural zoning, development impact fees, urban growth boundaries, and conservation easements. This book explores the use of another policy in some detail—preferential assessment of rural land under the real property tax. This tax policy is often called *use-value assessment* or *current-use assessment*.

Most citizens and even many tax professionals do not yet appreciate the important role that use-value assessment plays in our country's system of state and local taxation. The importance of UVA programs is illustrated in table 1.2. Over 61 percent of Ohio's total land area is enrolled in its Current Agricultural Use Value (CAUV) Program, for example. Some of the nation's most valuable farmland can be found in California, where the owners of more than fifteen million acres presently enjoy reduced property taxes under the state's Williamson Act Program. This tax policy has been in place in California since 1965. Use-value assessment is even a major facet of property taxation in tiny New Hampshire, where nearly three million acres (most of it forested) has been enrolled in the state's Current Use Program.

Tax preferences of this magnitude have major implications for the revenue-generating capacities of municipal governments and public school

TABLE 1.2
Extent of Use-Value Assessment Programs in Selected States

	Total Land Area (Millions of Acres)	Land in UVA Program (Millions of Acres)	UVA Land as Percentage of Total Land Area
California (2008)	101.0	15.69	15.5
New Hampshire (2010)	5.74	2.95	51.4
Ohio (2009)	26.21	16.13	61.5

SOURCES: CA Department of Conservation, *2010 Williamson Act Status Report*; NH Department of Revenue Administration, *2010 Current Use Report*; and Ohio Department of Taxation, *Taxable Current Agricultural Use Value (CAUV) of Real Property, Taxable Value of Real Property before CAUV, and Number of CAUV Acres and Parcels, by County, Calendar Year 2009*, table PD-32.

districts (Bowman, Cordes, and Metcalf 2009). Consider Ohio as an example. In the Buckeye state, numerous owners in both urban and rural counties enjoy major reductions in their property tax bills because of the CAUV Program. Table 1.3 shows that the differences between use-value assessments and market-value assessments are the greatest in the urban counties containing Cleveland (Cuyahoga County), Columbus (Franklin County), and Cincinnati (Hamilton County). Not only are the differences the greatest in those counties, but the ratio of use value to market values is the lowest in those counties. In Franklin County, for example, valuing UVA parcels at their current market value would result in assessments averaging more than $3,000 per acre. But enrollment in the CAUV Program reduces those assessments below market value by an average greater than $2,500 per acre. This implies both a substantial loss of property tax revenue going to local governments and also financial pressure on those localities to raise the tax rates that they levy on assessed property values to pay for local public services.

As shown in table 1.3, the reduction in assessed value per acre is significantly lower in the three largely rural counties of Darke, Hardin, and Seneca. However, an assessment reduction on CAUV parcels of $600 to $1,000 per acre still has a negative fiscal impact on local governments in counties with thousands of enrolled agricultural parcels.

TABLE 1.3
Current Ohio Agricultural Use-Value Program in Selected
Counties, 2009

	Number of Parcels	Average Parcel Size (acres)	Average Use Value per Acre ($)	Average Market Value per Acre ($)	Average Use Value per Acre as a Percent of Average Market Value (%)
Cuyahoga	189	12.3	1,064	5,924	18.0
Franklin	1,700	42.7	472	3,007	15.7
Hamilton	1,255	22.7	655	4,355	15.0
Darke	7,488	46.1	233	1,295	18.0
Hardin	5,351	51.7	196	759	25.8
Seneca	6,321	49.5	202	983	20.1

SOURCE: Ohio Department of Taxation, table PD-32.

Perhaps this tax preference for farmland could be justified if it actually worked to "save the family farmer," as was stated in many of the original policy discussions establishing this tax practice. However, one is struck by the small average size of CAUV parcels in urban and rural counties alike. Because the average farm size in Ohio is 185 acres, it is likely that many of these parcels are not commercially viable farms but rather are valuable pieces of developable real estate whose owners enjoy substantial property tax breaks because of the CAUV Program (U.S. Department of Agriculture 2007).

Despite their stated purpose of preserving rural lands from urban development, it is possible that UVA programs have had several unintended and negative consequences. One result is erosion of the legal and constitutional principle of *uniformity of taxation*, an issue that will be addressed in chapter 2. Another is shifting of the local tax burden to other property owners, perhaps in a regressive manner. According to the Texas Comptroller of Public Accounts, use-value appraisal of farm, ranch, and forested lands reduces the property tax base in Texas by more than $2.9 billion, a whopping sum even in the Lone Star state. The resulting shift in the property tax burden to other property owners costs low- and middle-income households hundreds of dollars annually (Combs 2013). Chapters 3 and 4 will discuss this issue of tax incidence and other policy questions.

Although UVA programs operate largely outside public view, they do occasionally generate political controversy and even legislative action. Concern about "fake farmers" who enjoy low property tax bills has been a simmering issue in New Jersey for two decades. The 1964 Farmland Assessment Act allowed landowners with as few as five acres and who sold $500 or more of farm or horticultural products during each of the previous two years to lower their land assessments to as little as $27 per acre. Christie Whitman came under fire during her tenure as New Jersey's governor for reducing property taxes on her two estates by selling firewood to relatives and friends. Former state senator Ellen Karcher also attracted criticism for saving tens of thousands of dollars in annual property taxes by selling a few Christmas trees each year.

Examples such as these prompted a bipartisan effort in the New Jersey legislature to reform the state's farmland assessment program to prevent participation by those who are not truly farmers. Senate Bill 589, which passed by a unanimous vote of 39–0 in June 2012, proposed raising the annual revenue threshold from farming activity to $1,000 and called for a review of that sales threshold every three years by the State Farmland Evaluation Committee. It also proposed a $5,000 fine for fraudulent participation in the UVA program. Governor Chris Christie signed these provisions into law in April 2013. (Recent trends in certified organic and community-supported agriculture, two types of farming that make use of relatively small land areas and generate low levels of revenue, could complicate efforts to identify "true farmer" thresholds.) Chapter 5 surveys criticisms of UVA as it has been practiced for 50 years and offers several reforms of UVA programs that governors and legislators might want to consider for adoption.

2 \ History, Design, and Features

The adoption of UVA programs in the United States was driven principally by a combination of two factors: rapid urbanization and rising land values relative to farm income. Additional factors related to tax assessment practice also contributed to UVA adoption. This chapter tells the story of the diffusion of UVA programs across the country.

Many people are aware that the expansion of U.S. metropolitan regions after World War II resulted in the development of tens of millions of acres of farm, ranch, forest, and other rural lands. Berry and Plaut (1978), for example, estimated that an annual average of 902,000 acres in the United States had been converted from rural to urban uses between 1959 and 1969. More recently, Alig, Pantinga, Ahn, and Kline (2003) have estimated that the nation's developed area more than doubled between 1960 and 1997, from 25.5 to 65.5 million acres. An influential 1981 report issued jointly by the U.S. Department of Agriculture and the President's Council on Environmental Quality (USDA-CEQ) noted the "major transition" in land use under way at that time. The authors of this report recommended that "the federal government make the protection of good agricultural land a national policy" (6, 15).[1]

---

1. Decisions about land use in the United States were then and still are primarily private ones regulated by state and local policies. However, purchases of U.S. farmland by foreign citizens were a federal policy concern at that time. That concern contributed to enactment of the Foreign Investment in Real Property Tax Act of 1980.

Published claims about the rate of land development need to be taken with one or more grains of salt, however. As Bills (2007, 167) has observed, federal data sources on land use and land conversion frequently "conflict with each other." Even more pointedly, Fischel (1982) has concluded that the 1981 USDA-CEQ study, for a number of technical reasons, seriously exaggerated the rate of farmland development that had occurred. One reason is that the method used by the Soil Conservation Service to measure urban land area changed between its 1958 study and the one it conducted in 1977. Hence, one cannot simply take the difference between the two reported urban-area measures to determine the increase in urbanized area over those two decades.

The most recent and reliable data on land use change in the United States come from the USDA Natural Resources Conservation Service (2013). In table 1 of its *2007 National Resources Inventory*, cropland acreage in the contiguous 48 states fell by 14.90 percent from 1982 to 2007. During that same time period, the extent of pastureland in those states dropped by 9.38 percent.[2] From 1982 to 2007, the amount of developed land in the United States increased by 56.78 percent, to more than 111 million acres.

Regardless of the precise extent to which land has been developed in the United States since 1945, the acreage converted from rural use during that period has been substantial. This expansion of metropolitan regions into the countryside helped to launch a political movement from the 1960s through the 1980s that favored preferential assessment of rural land. In his major study of use-value farmland assessment for the International Association of Assessing Officers, Gloudemans (1974, 10) argued that this movement was motivated by "two major concerns: (1) concern for the economic viability of the farmer; and (2) concern over land use and the environment."[3]

---

2. Not all of this decline in cropland and pastureland was due to urbanization, however. During that 25-year period, the acreage of forests in the United States grew slightly (0.75 percent), and nearly 33 million acres of rural land entered the federal Conservation Reserve Program.

3. Concerns about preserving family farmers were sometimes intertwined with concerns about conserving prime agricultural lands and ensuring future food supplies. See Gardner (1977) for an analysis of these issues.

The first concern was that farmers on the metropolitan fringe faced growing property tax burdens for a pair of reasons. One is that newly arriving households and businesses demanded higher municipal service levels. The other reason is that farmland prices and land value assessments escalated because of the increasing development potential of rural parcels. A study by Blase and Staub (1971) supports Gloudemans' general point about the escalating property tax bills faced by some farmers during the post–World War II era. In their study of seven counties in the metro Kansas City region during the early 1960s, the authors found a higher level and more rapid growth of property tax per acre in the more suburban and urban counties of the region. They also found that "the proportion of gross farm income absorbed by the property tax was approximately four times greater in the urban county than the average for the entire study area" (1971, 173). Hence, support for preferential assessment of rural land was sometimes framed as a measure to protect family farmers and ranchers from financial pressure and even ruin.[4]

The second concern mentioned by Gloudemans was the fear that growth of metropolitan regions would destroy wetland and forest ecosystems, eliminate wildlife habitats and scenic vistas, or otherwise degrade environmental values: "Environmentalists . . . contend that these remaining [rural] lands . . . will be swept away in the tide of urban sprawl unless afforded some protection" (1974, 12). This second argument for preferential assessment of rural lands seems to presuppose that private land ownership and a competitive land market will fail to produce the socially efficient amount of rural land preservation (Gardner 1977).

Although it cannot be proved that the state legislators and conservationists who supported enactment of preferential assessment of rural land actually used "market failure" arguments to make their case, it is clear

---

4. Writing during the period when UVA programs were being launched, Conklin and Lesher (1977) argued that financial pressure on farmers near the fringe of metropolitan regions also results in "premature and excessive" disinvestment in soil fertility and land improvements. Their argument is unconvincing, however, since it is hard to understand why a farmer should make a substantial gross investment in the agricultural potential of a land parcel if he anticipates selling to a developer within a few years.

that some academic writers of that era were ready to follow this line of argument. Veseth (1979, 98), for example, commented as follows: "Agricultural and open lands are particularly susceptible to development pressures . . . because they generate positive externalities. . . . The landowners' benefits are largely financial. They receive the profits from the crops, timber, and livestock that are raised on their land. The public's benefits are largely nonfinancial . . . [and include] the aesthetic, recreational, and ecological services which open lands provide." Since the annual benefits to society from a parcel of undeveloped land arguably exceed those captured by the parcel's private owner, some form of state intervention to preserve rural land may be justified.[5] Whether the appropriate form of public intervention is preferential assessment of certain categories of rural land for purposes of property taxation is a question addressed in the remainder of this book.

Enactment of Use-Value Assessment Programs

During the 1960s and 1970s, dozens of state governments enacted use-value assessment programs for specific categories of rural land.[6] This nationwide wave of state tax reform began in Maryland in 1957. That starting point can be explained, at least in part, by two empirical facts. One is that large swaths of Maryland farmland were converted to suburban uses immediately after World War II. In 1957, for example, William Levitt, the New York homebuilder, purchased a 2,226-acre farm dating to colonial times in order to construct six thousand suburban homes near the nation's capital (United Press 1957; Forstall 1995). From 1940 to 1960, the populations of Montgomery and Prince George's counties quadrupled, whereas the population of Baltimore County more than tripled (U.S. Census Bureau 2011).

Associated with this rapid suburbanization of Washington, DC, and Baltimore City, there was a 330 percent increase in the ratio of farmland

---

5. Lopez, Shah, and Altobello (1994) make a similar argument.

6. For a brief summary of UVA legislation up to the early 1970s, see Barlowe, Ahl, and Bachman (1973). For another legislative summary that focuses on southern states up to the early 1980s, see Rodgers and Williams (1983).

prices to net farm income in Maryland from 1950 to 1971 (Gloudemans 1974). This pair of facts helps us to understand the 1957 action taken by the Maryland legislature that was intended to protect the state's remaining farmland from development.

The rapid spread of UVA programs to other states cannot be understood, however, simply by looking at state population growth and farm income data during that era. Brigham (1980) offers a fascinating historical sketch of how the local property tax had been administered in many states before 1957. He points out that local assessors frequently gave de facto tax preferences to farmers (and homeowners) despite state constitutional provisions requiring uniformity and equality of taxation. These assessment practices were intended to provide property tax relief to "deserving citizens" but resulted in dramatic differences in assessment ratios among taxable properties within the same jurisdiction.[7]

After World War II, the expansion of state aid programs required the use of numerical formulas to distribute state grants to counties, cities, towns, and school districts. Property wealth per resident or pupil often played a major role in those state aid formulas. Thus, pressure mounted at the state level for uniform assessment practices within and among localities in order to ensure an equitable distribution of state grants. The subsequent elimination of de facto tax preferences at the local level of government resulted in higher property tax bills for many rural landowners and fueled efforts to gain de jure tax preferences for agricultural and forest properties. Hence, efforts to launch use-value assessment programs were often a political reaction to recent trends in both real estate markets and state and local intergovernmental relations.

Despite these two national trends of suburbanization and rural land price growth, the introduction of use-value assessment of rural land faced a serious legal obstacle in a number of states. As Coe (2009) has pointed out, uniformity is perhaps the most commonly stated principle of taxation that is embodied in state constitutional law. In general, the principle of uniformity requires that tax laws be applied in an identical manner to all

7. A property's assessment ratio is its assessed value for tax purposes divided by its market value during the same period of observation.

similarly situated taxpayers. Thirty-nine states have an explicit uniformity provision in their constitutions. (See appendix 2.1 for a list of these states.) The spirit of uniform taxation is well expressed in the West Virginia state constitution:

> Subject to the exceptions in this section contained, taxation shall be equal and uniform throughout the state, and all property, both real and personal, shall be taxed in proportion to its value to be ascertained as directed by law. No one species of property from which a tax may be collected shall be taxed higher than any other species of property of equal value. (Article 10–1)

Because preferential assessment of rural land violates this uniformity principle, a number of states had to amend their state constitutions before they could enact and implement use-value assessment programs. Because of constitutional provisions allowing differential taxation of different property classes, enactment of UVA statutes was sufficient in other states— Nebraska, for example. In such cases, uniformity applies within each class, but not across classes of property.

Of course, the politics of adopting use-value assessment varied across states and through the decades. The following subsections describe the political history of UVA adoption in five states ranging in size and location from Hawaii to Wisconsin.

Use-value assessment in California

California was one of the early adopters of current-use assessment of rural land.[8] In 1965, its legislature passed the California Land Conservation Act (CLCA), commonly known as the Williamson Act. The stated goals of this statute were to preserve agricultural lands in order to ensure adequate food supply, to discourage premature conversion of land to urban uses, and to preserve agricultural land for its open-space amenity value. The Williamson Act enables counties and cities to designate agricultural preserves and then offer preferential property taxation based on agricultural

---

8. The sources for this section are Schwartz, Hansen, and Foin (1975) and www .consrv.ca.gov/dlrp/lca/Pages/Index.aspx.

use-value in return for a contract barring land development for a minimum of 10 years. After the first decade of the contract, there is an automatic extension every year unless the owner or the county files a notice of
contract nonrenewal. If such a notice is filed, then the property's assessment ratio rises incrementally until it reaches unity when the contract finally terminates after nine years. An immediate termination of a Williamson contract is also possible but only if permitted by the city or county
government and if the owner pays a penalty equal to 12.5 percent of market value.

As of 2010, all but four of California's counties had chosen to partici-
pate in the Williamson Act Program. At the beginning of 2009, half of the
state's farmland and almost 30 percent of its privately owned acreage had
been enrolled in the program. A program of this magnitude must have significant effects on both rural land markets and local government budgets in
the Golden State.

The 1972 Open Space Subvention Act modifies the impact of the Williamson Act on local government budgets by providing state grants to
partially replace forgone local property tax revenues. From 1972 through
2008, those subvention payments from Sacramento to the cities and counties totaled $839 million and were financed in large measure by growing
state income tax revenue. Subvention payments were suspended during
2009, however, because of the state's mammoth budget deficit.[9]

---

9. The passage of the Proposition 13 property tax limitation in 1978 was another major change to the tax system in California. Sexton, Sheffrin, and O'Sullivan
(1999) make the case that passage of Proposition 13 is not surprising in retrospect. In
the 1970s, rapidly rising property values and stable tax rates were responsible for dramatically higher property taxes as a share of income. At the same time, the State of
California was accumulating a projected budget surplus of nearly $10 billion. State
and local governments did not respond to rising property values and accumulating
state revenues by reducing tax rates. Hence, voters took the initiative and passed
Proposition 13, which capped the property tax rate at 1 percent; rolled back assessed
values to their 1975–1976 levels and limited assessed value increases thereafter to
2 percent; and required reassessment at market value upon property sale, effectively
converting the property tax system to an acquisition value system. Research is needed
on how the Williamson Act and Proposition 13 have interacted and what their joint
impact on land use patterns has been.

Use-value assessment in Hawaii

In 1961, the newly admitted state of Hawaii passed its comprehensive Land Use Law.[10] This act created a nine-member Land Use Commission (LUC) that was empowered to assign all land in the state to four categories: urban, rural, agricultural, and conservation. The LUC was also made responsible for establishing and adjusting the boundaries of those four districts. County governments, the LUC, and the State Board of Land and Natural Resources share jurisdiction over land uses across the islands. According to Mark, Yamauchi, and Okimoto (1982, 95), this "represents the most comprehensive statewide land use control system in the United States."

The motivating force behind passage of the Hawaii Land Use Law was a desire to retain prime farmlands in agricultural use in the face of rapid urbanization and growth of tourism.[11] Hence, the act required the state's Department of Taxation to assess farmland according to its current-use value (even if the acreage fell outside the boundary of an agricultural district). For historical reasons, ownership of agricultural land is highly concentrated in Hawaii, and sales of working agricultural properties are rare. Hence, assessment of rural lands has had to rely on income-capitalization methods and on lease-rental data as proxies for farm income.

Use-value assessment in Nevada

At the beginning of the 1970s, de facto preferential assessment of farms and ranches was common in Nevada.[12] Some Nevadans feared a taxpayer suit demanding market-value assessment of rural lands based on the uniform and equal taxation clause of the state constitution. Several farm associations actively supported adoption of an amendment to make current-

---

10. The sources for this section are Mark, Yamauchi, and Okimoto (1982) and http://luc.state.hi.us/about.htm.

11. Rapid growth of population and tourism in Honolulu inspired Joni Mitchell's 1970 "Big Yellow Taxi" lyric, "They paved paradise and put up a parking lot."

12. The sources for this section are Atkinson (1977) and www.census.gov /population/www/censusdata/cencounts/files/nv190090.txt.

use assessment of farm and ranch lands constitutional. Support among ranchers was mixed, however, because of the rollback provision of the proposed amendment. This clause provided that the owner of rural land who had enjoyed lower property taxes because of use-value assessment would have to pay a penalty equal to several years of tax savings if and when the parcel was developed for urban use.

There was also urban support for an amendment allowing use-value assessment of farm and ranch land. Conservationists in Las Vegas and Reno feared that assessing rural land according to its current market value would accelerate urban development. The nearly sixfold increase in the population of Clark County from 1950 to 1970 helped to fuel this anxiety about urban sprawl (even though much of Nevada was uninhabited then and remains so today). In the November 1974 referendum that endorsed use-value assessment, there was majority support in the two urban counties but in only three of the fifteen rural counties of the state.

Use-value assessment in Texas

Implementation of current-use assessment has been a protracted legal process in Texas.[13] The constitutional amendment of 1966 was restrictive in several respects. For example, it provided that only farm and ranch land owned by a "natural person" qualified for a property tax preference. That is, farms and ranches owned by corporations or partnerships and all timberland regardless of ownership did not qualify for lower property taxes.[14] A dozen years later, a second amendment to the Texas constitution enlarged the potential for use-value assessment in the state. Implementation, however, awaited passage of HB1060 during May, 1979.

---

13. The source for this section is Hickman and Crowther (1991).

14. The issue of corporate farming also arose at this time, with a number of states passing anticorporate farming laws in order to support family farming and prevent perceived environmental and other abuses associated with corporate farming. For a state-by-state review of these laws, see the Community Environmental Legal Defense Fund on Anti-Corporate Farming Laws in the Heartland, http://celdf.org/anti-corporate-farming-laws-in-the-heartland.

At the end of the 1970s, forested and "ecological laboratory" lands became qualifying uses. The 1978 amendment increased eligibility to include qualifying land owned by corporations, partnerships, and other legal entities except when nonresident aliens or foreign governments held a majority interest. The later amendment increased the rollback tax period from three to five years but cut the interest rate applied to back taxes from 12 to 7 percent when a land parcel no longer qualified for use-value assessment. The second amendment also required that the income-capitalization method be used to estimate use values of qualifying properties.

Use-value assessment in Wisconsin

From 1848 until 1974, the state constitution in Wisconsin required uniform taxation of all property.[15] That situation changed with the 1974 amendment to the uniformity clause that allowed nonuniform taxation of agricultural and other undeveloped land. Not until 1993, however, did the legislature direct the Department of Revenue (DOR) to study the implementation of use-value assessment of farmland. One possible reason for this late interest in UVA adoption is that Wisconsin farmers had already enjoyed a circuit breaker form of tax relief tied to the state income tax.

In 1995, Wisconsin Act 27 provided for use-value assessment to be implemented over a phase-in period of 10 years. The assessed value of agricultural land was to be frozen at its 1995 levels during 1996 and 1997. Then the assessed value of farmland was to be reduced by 10 percent annually from its 1995 levels through 2007. This act also created the Farmland Advisory Council to advise DOR on use-value assessment methods and to recommend a penalty for conversion of agricultural land to other uses.

The pace of property tax reform in Wisconsin accelerated in 1999. Act 9 established a conversion penalty equal to the difference between taxes owed under market valuation and taxes paid under agricultural-use valuation for the two years prior to land conversion. An emergency rule issued

---

15. The sources for this section are Boldt (2002) and Youngman (2005). See also Wisconsin Department of Revenue (2010).

by DOR suspended the phase-in process and implemented complete use-value assessment effective January 1, 2000.

In 2001, Act 109 changed the land-conversion penalty to an amount per acre specific to each county. This amount was 5–10 percent of the difference between a county's average market price of farmland and the average use-value of an agricultural acre in that county. In 2002, the Wisconsin Supreme Court upheld early implementation of use-value assessment. During the following year, Act 33 redefined classes of taxable property to include agricultural forestland, a class to be assessed at 50 percent of market value.

Characteristics of UVA Programs

With the widespread diffusion of use-value assessment programs across the United States, it is helpful to look at the similarities and differences among those state programs in order to learn how UVA has been implemented and whether it is effective in reaching its policy objectives.

One important feature of UVA program design is how easy it is for rural landowners to file the paperwork to enroll their properties. As appendix 2.2 demonstrates, the application requirements are relatively simple in most states. Of the 18 state or county jurisdictions surveyed in the appendix, nearly all require submission of an application form no longer than two pages. However, some states also require attachment of supporting documents such as federal tax returns, detailed property maps, or forest management plans. New York stands out as a state requiring a fairly long application (five pages, to be exact) for use-value assessment of agricultural land.

This simplicity of the application process in most jurisdictions has certainly encouraged enrollment in UVA programs, especially by owners of smaller rural properties that qualify for inclusion. In those states that impose a development penalty when rural land no longer qualifies for UVA, a main purpose of the application form seems to be informing owners about the financial consequences of future land development before they enroll in the program. In some states—Nebraska, for example—the application form is very terse and does not require evidence to verify that

TABLE 2.1
Use-Value Assessment Acreage Minimums, Selected States

	Agricultural Land	Timber Land
3 acres	Louisiana, Maryland	Louisiana
5 acres	Idaho, Maine, Massachusetts, North Carolina, Rhode Island	Idaho, Maryland
7 acres	New York	
10 acres	Delaware, Kentucky, Minnesota, New Hampshire, Ohio, Pennsylvania	Delaware, Kentucky, Massachusetts, New Hampshire, Pennsylvania, West Virginia
15 acres	Tennessee	Montana, Tennessee
20 acres	Nevada, South Dakota, Washington	Minnesota, North Carolina
25 acres	Vermont	
160 acres	Montana	

SOURCE: State statutes cited in appendix 2.3.

NOTE: Smaller acreages are eligible for enrollment in some of these states if the owner provides evidence that the property generates at least a minimum amount of sales revenue or gross income from its current use.

newly enrolled properties actually meet state criteria for enrollment. Verification is up to the local property tax assessor.

Of greater importance than the length of the application form are the eligibility criteria that qualify some rural properties but not others for enrollment in UVA programs. A common eligibility requirement is that a parcel meets or exceeds a certain minimum acreage to qualify for the state's program. What is striking about these acreage minimums is how small they are in most states. As table 2.1 shows, parcels as small as three or five acres qualify for UVA in some states. It is unlikely that parcels so small can be commercially viable sources of crops, livestock, or timber. Montana appears to be exceptional in requiring a sizable acreage to enroll a farm or ranch for preferential tax assessment.

Another common eligibility requirement for agricultural UVA is that the owner needs to document or at least attest that the property has generated at least a minimum amount of gross income or sales revenues from agricultural activities during recent years. As table 2.2 demonstrates, this commercial agriculture minimum is quite modest in most states. Hence, many owners of parcels that qualify for agricultural UVA are not full-time farmers who rely on farming for their livelihood. These owners are sometimes referred to as "hobby farmers" or "gentleman farmers" in popular parlance. Minimum income requirements would clearly enable states to favor large parcels of land and discriminate against small parcels.

In some states, but not most, a parcel that previously qualified for UVA can lose its eligibility prior to an actual physical change in land use if there is evidence that the property will or might be developed in the near future. In Arizona, an undeveloped property is no longer eligible for preferential assessment if there has been an application to re-zone the parcel for urban use, recording of a subdivision plat, or recent installation of survey stakes or utility services. In Indiana, rezoning of an enrolled property or its subdivision disqualifies the land for continued use-value assessment. In Nebraska, rural land that is now within the boundaries of any sanitary or improvement district or a city is ineligible unless subject to a conservation easement. In North Dakota, a complex set of criteria described in appendix 2.3 can disqualify farmland parcels platted after 1981.

What happens if the owner of a rural parcel enjoys lower property taxes for a number of years because of UVA enrollment but then develops the parcel for a residential, commercial, or industrial use? Since the property no longer qualifies for preferential assessment, its assessed value will increase quite substantially, and the owner will owe significantly higher property taxes on the parcel's land value in years to come. But will the land-owner bear any additional financial consequences for converting his or her property from a qualifying rural use to a developed use? Will the owner face a development penalty after benefiting from years of reduced property taxes because of UVA enrollment?

The answers to these questions depend very much on the specific UVA statute and administrative rules that a state has adopted. As shown in table 2.3, 21 states do not levy a development penalty on some or all parcels that have been enrolled in a UVA program when those parcels lose their eligibility for preferential assessment.

TABLE 2.2
Farm Income or Sales Requirement for UVA Enrollment,
Selected States

Alaska	Owner or lessee derives at least 10 percent of annual gross income from farming.
Delaware	Gross sales of agricultural or forestry products of at least $1,000 per year during the two preceding years.
Kauai County, Hawaii	Filing of IRS Schedule F from previous year documenting profit or loss from farming.
Maine	Gross farm income of at least $2,000 per year during one of two preceding years.
Maryland	Average gross farm income of at least $2,500 if under 20 acres.
Massachusetts	At least $500 of annual sales receipts from farming activity.
Montana	Over half of owner's Montana gross income derives from agriculture and minimum of $1,500.
New Jersey	Gross annual sales of $1,000 for first five acres plus average of $5 per acre for each acre over the first five.
New York	Annual gross farm sales of $10,000 or more during preceding two years.
North Carolina	Average gross farm income of at least $1,000 during preceding three years.
Ohio	Average gross income of at least $2,500.
Oregon	Gross income of at least $3,000 if 30 or more acres. Smaller income amounts if smaller parcels of farmland.
Pennsylvania	At least $2,000 of gross farm income during the previous three years.
Rhode Island	At least $2,500 of gross farm income during one of last two years.
South Dakota	At least one-third of total family gross income from farming.
Tennessee	Gross income from farm sales, farm rent, or federal farm support payments averaging $1,500 per year over three-year period.
Texas	Agriculture as primary occupation of owner and primary source of income.

SOURCE: Statutes cited in appendix 2.3.

TABLE 2.3
States with No UVA Development Penalty

Arizona	Iowa	Nebraska
Arkansas	Kansas	New Mexico
Colorado (agricultural land)	Kentucky	North Dakota
Florida	Louisiana	Oklahoma
Idaho (agricultural land)	Mississippi	South Dakota
Illinois (farm and forestland)	Missouri	West Virginia
Indiana (agricultural land)	Montana	Wyoming

SOURCE: Statutes cited in appendix 2.3.

In the remaining 28 states with UVA programs, landowners are subject to development penalties when their properties no longer qualify for preferential assessment.[16] These states have adopted some variant of either a rollback tax or a conveyance tax to recapture some of the property taxes forgone during the years of program enrollment and to discourage parcel development. Rollback taxes typically recover several years of property tax savings, or property taxes deferred, because of use-value assessment. In some states, those deferred property taxes are subject to interest charges as well.

Conveyance taxes apply a tax rate to the market value of the land parcel during the year when it no longer qualifies for preferential assessment. This tax rate varies inversely in some states with the number of years that a parcel has been enrolled in the UVA program. Massachusetts is unusual in that it has both rollback and conveyance tax provisions in its UVA statutes.[17]

Table 2.4 summarizes the penalty provisions in the states with rollback taxes. Note that states vary significantly in the number of years of deferred taxes that the owner of a disqualified parcel owes to the state or local government. The deterrent to land development is presumably stron-

---

16. In Hawaii, the development penalty varies by county. See appendix 2.3 for details.

17. In addition to its rollback penalty, Massachusetts imposes a conveyance tax with a rate as high as 10 percent if a disqualifying use occurs during the first decade of classification.

TABLE 2.4
States with UVA Rollback Penalties

Alabama
3 years of deferred taxes

Alaska
7 years of deferred taxes
plus 8 percent interest

Colorado
7 years of deferred taxes for
conservation easement land

Delaware
10 years of deferred taxes

Georgia
Deferred taxes plus interest
with years declining with
period of enrollment

Idaho
Up to 10 years of deferred
taxes for forestland

Illinois
3 years of deferred taxes
plus 5 percent interest for
open space land

Indiana
Up to 10 years of deferred
taxes plus 10 percent
interest on forestland

Maine
5 years of deferred interest
plus interest on agricultural
land

Massachusetts
5 years of deferred taxes
plus 5 percent interest

Minnesota
3 years of deferred
taxes

Nevada
Deferred taxes for current
and 6 previous years

New Jersey
Deferred taxes for current
and 2 previous years

New York
5X taxes saved in most
recent year plus 6 percent
interest

North Carolina
Deferred taxes for current
and 3 previous years plus
interest

Ohio
Deferred taxes for 3
previous years

Oregon
Deferred taxes for 5 or
10 years

Pennsylvania
7 years of deferred taxes
plus 6 percent interest

South Carolina
Deferred taxes for current
and 5 preceding years

Tennessee
3 years of deferred taxes for
agricultural and forest
parcels; 5 years for open
space parcels

Texas
3 years of deferred taxes
plus interest for farmland;
5 years for open space land

Utah
Maximum of 5 years of
deferred taxes

Virginia
5 years of deferred taxes
plus interest, with local
option to modify penalty

Washington
7 years of deferred taxes
plus interest plus additional
20 percent of that total

Wisconsin
Complicated rollback
described in appendix 2.3

SOURCE: Statutes cited in appendix 2.3.

TABLE 2.5
States with UVA Conveyance Penalties

California	*New Hampshire*
12.5 percent of market value of land parcel, with local option for higher percentage	10 percent of market value of land parcel
Connecticut	*Rhode Island*
10 percent of market value of land parcel within one year of classification, with tax rate falling to zero after 10 years	10 percent of market value of land parcel if 6 or fewer years of classification with tax rate falling to zero after 15 years
Maryland	*Vermont*
Tax rate of 3 to 5 percent of sales price for agricultural land, with rate based on parcel size and condition	10 percent of market value if classification for more than 10 years; 20 percent if 10 or fewer years

SOURCE: Statutes cited in appendix 2.3.

ger in those states that collect more years of deferred taxes if development occurs. Table 2.5 summarizes the penalty provisions in states with conveyance taxes. Note that these states are clustered along the East Coast or West Coast, not in the agricultural heartland of the nation.

Beginning in Maryland in the 1950s, UVA programs diffused across the United States during the last half of the twentieth century. Nearly all states now offer use-value assessment to some or all of the owners of agricultural land. A substantial number also offer preferential assessment to owners of timberland. UVA eligibility of rural parcels for conservation, open space, or recreational purposes is less common.

Applying for the tax benefits of UVA enrollment is relatively straightforward in most states. However, states vary widely in how severe the penalties are, if any, when a parcel is withdrawn from the UVA program for development. Twenty-one states do not penalize the development of agricultural land at all. Vermont, on the other hand, collects a penalty equal to 20 percent of market value if a rural parcel has been enrolled as a UVA property for 10 years or less. As we shall see in the following chapters, the diversity of state UVA programs generates important evidence about how these programs perform and how they might be improved.

APPENDIX 2.1
States with Constitutional Provisions Requiring Uniform Taxation

Alabama	Indiana	Nevada	South Dakota
Arizona	Kansas	New Jersey	Tennessee
Arkansas	Kentucky	New Mexico	Texas
California	Louisiana	North Carolina	Utah
Colorado	Maryland	North Dakota	Virginia
Delaware	Michigan	Ohio	Washington
Florida	Minnesota	Oklahoma	West Virginia
Georgia	Mississippi	Oregon	Wisconsin
Idaho	Missouri	Pennsylvania	Wyoming
Illinois	Nebraska	South Carolina	

SOURCE: Coe (2009, 159–160).

APPENDIX 2.2
Use-Value Assessment Application Process

	Number of Pages	UVA Category	Submission to:
Arizona (Form 82916)	1	Agricultural	County assessor
	Required Information: Parcel ID number, acreage, affirmation of eligibility		
Connecticut (Form M-29)	1–2	Agricultural	Town assessor
	Required Information: Property location, gross farm income, type of farm operation, sketch of property with soil types, acknowledgment of development penalty		
Kauai, Hawaii (Form P-41)	1	Agricultural	County assessor
	Required Information: Acreage, specific land use, contract length, lease details, acknowledgment of development penalty		
Georgia (Form PT-230)	1	Agricultural	County assessor
	Required Information: Acreages by agricultural purpose, parcel ID number, individual or corporate owners, affirmation of bona fide commercial agricultural use, acknowledgment of development penalty		

	Number of Pages	UVA Category	Submission to:
Idaho	1.5	Timber harvesting	County assessor
	Required Information: Acreage, parcel ID number, affirmation of intent to commercially harvest trees, 10-year minimum contract period, acknowledgment of development penalty, authorization to examine land and records		
Jefferson County, Kentucky	1	Agricultural	County assessor
	Required Information: Acreage, parcel ID number, individual or corporate owner, affirmation of agricultural use		
Massachusetts (Form CL-1)	2	Agricultural, forest, or recreational	Town assessor
	Required Information: Parcel ID number, total acreage, UVA category, specific agricultural or rec uses, federal & state income tax forms, land uses of past two years, lease information, acknowledgment of rights and obligations		
Maryland	1	Agricultural	Regional office of Maryland Department of Assessments & Taxation
	Required Information: Total acreage and specific agricultural uses, quantities of last harvest for each crop, gross sales if farm < 5 acres, lease information, federal Schedule F, acknowledgment of development penalty		
Maine (Form PTF-475)	2	Agricultural	Town assessor
	Required Information: Parcel ID number, acreage, and breakdown by specific agricultural use (including forest), gross farm income for past 2 or 5 years, map of property, acknowledgment of development penalty		
Montana (Form AB-3)	3	Agricultural	Montana Department of Revenue office
	Required Information: Legal description of property, actual farm output and gross farm income of past year, on-farm consumption, lease information, covenants restricting agricultural use, acreages for specific agricultural uses		

(*continued*)

	Number of Pages	UVA Category	Submission to:
Nebraska (Form 456)	1	Agricultural	County assessor

Required Information: Parcel ID number, total acres and area devoted to agricultural use, affirmation of eligibility

	Number of Pages	UVA Category	Submission to:
New Hampshire (Form A-10)	2	Farm, forest, unproductive or wet land	Town assessor

Required Information: Parcel ID number, map of property and specific uses, acknowledgment of development penalty, signatures of majority of town selectmen, soil potential data, forest management plan (if any)

New Jersey (Form FA-1)	1	Agricultural	Local assessor

Required Information: Names of owner and operator, parcel ID number, current acreages devoted to extensive list of particular crops and livestock or to federal conservation programs or to renewable energy, owner informed about development penalty

New York (Form RP-305)	5	Agricultural	Local assessor (except Nassau and Tompkins counties)

Required Information: Tax map number, acres for specific agricultural purposes, gross sales for newly established farm operations, name of renter, acres by mineral soil group, acknowledgment of development penalty

Oregon (Form 150-309-024)	2	Forestland	County assessor

Required Information: Parcel ID number, acquisition date, map, affirmation of tree harvesting as "predominant purpose," forest management plan (if any), acknowledgment of development penalty, information about subdivision or easements suggesting other uses

Fairfax County, Virginia	2	Agricultural or forestal district	Fairfax Department of Tax Administration

Required Information: Parcel ID number, acres in agricultural or forest use above minimums, description of structures, five consecutive years of commercial farm use or presence of commercially valuable trees, acknowledgment of development penalty

	Number of Pages	UVA Category	Submission to:
Vermont (Form LU-AFCFB)	1	Agricultural, forest, and conservation	Vermont Department of Taxes
		Required Information: Acres and qualified uses of land, number of farm buildings, description and map of property location, specific agricultural uses, acknowledgment of development penalty	
Washington (Chapter 84.34 RCW)	1.5	Agricultural	County assessor
		Required Information: Parcel ID number, acres in specific agricultural uses, rental or lease agreement, description of improvements, primary residence, map showing uses, yield and gross income data for past 5 years if fewer than 20 acres, acknowledgment of development penalty	

SOURCE: UVA application forms from various state governments.

APPENDIX 2.3
Characteristics of State UVA Programs

ALABAMA

Relevant Statutes:
Ala. Code § 40-7-25.1, Ala. Code § 40-7-25.3

Eligible Uses:
Agricultural/Farmland; Forest/Timber Production

Eligibility Requirements:
In order for property to qualify for current-use valuation, the property must be Class III Property, which is defined as follows: All agricultural, forest, and residential property, and historic buildings and sites.

AGRICULTURAL AND FOREST PROPERTY. All real property used for raising, harvesting, and selling crops or for the feeding, breeding, management, raising, sale of, or the production of livestock, including beef cattle, sheep, swine, horses, ponies, mules, poultry, fur-bearing animals, honeybees, and fish, or for dairying and the sale of dairy products, or for the growing and sale of timber and forest products, or any other agricultural or horticultural use or animal husbandry and any combination thereof.

Method of UV Assessment:
Tax assessor determines productivity rating or ratings applicable to property utilizing defined soil groups. The income method is used. The Department of Revenue,

utilizing statistics from various sources listed, determines the current-use standard value for agricultural property. Steps include determining state's top three crops in terms of acreage harvested for most recent calendar year, calculating gross return per crop per year using seasonal average price received for these crops in the 10 most recent calendar years. The cost of production of each crop is subtracted, giving the net return to land per year per crop. The values of net return are totaled in a weighted fashion with respect to average number of acres of each crop being harvested in the state in the 10 most recent calendar years. Income flow per acre is capitalized by dividing it by the average federal bank loans charged by the New Orleans District Federal Land Bank for the 10 most recent calendar years since 1973. Rate is reduced by 4.5 percent for first year lesser of 4.5 percent or difference of the FLB – 2 percent, whichever is less. The figure obtained is increased by 20 percent for productivity rating of good, 0 percent for average, –30 percent for poor, and –75 percent for nonproductive. Additional lower and upper bounds on value determined per acre.

Development Penalty:
When sold or converted to nonqualified use, "the tax assessor shall compute the amount of ad valorem property taxes that would have been payable with respect to such converted property if the sales price or the fair and reasonable market value of such property at the time of its conversion, whichever is greater, had been used instead of the current use value of such property in computing the amount of taxes payable with respect to such property for each of the three ad valorem tax years preceding the tax year beginning on the October 1 next succeeding the conversion of such property."

ALASKA

Relevant Statutes:
Alaska Stat. § 29.45.060; Alaska Admin. Code tit. 3 § 138.010 ~ § 138.020 (in effect for 2010)

Eligible Uses:
Agricultural/Farmland

Eligibility Requirements:
"'Farm use' means the use of land for profit for raising and harvesting crops, for the feeding, breeding, and management of livestock, for dairying, or another agricultural use, or any combination of these. To be farm use land, the owner or lessee must be actively engaged in farming the land, and derive at least 10 percent of yearly gross income from the land."

"In the event of a crop failure by an act of God the previous year, the owner or lessee may submit an affidavit affirming that 10 percent of gross income for the past three years was from farming."

Method of UV Assessment:
"Agricultural land in Alaska is valued at market value as evidenced by the market. We do not use production rates based on soil types or other methodology as used by

other states. Our statutes require Ag land to be based on market value as Ag land, as opposed to the highest and best use." —Steve Van Sant, state assessor

Recent Use Values ($ per acre):
Average use value of $1,262 in 2012, 76 percent below market value.

Development Penalty:
Rollback tax + 8 percent interest for preceding seven years. "If the land is sold, leased, or otherwise disposed of for uses incompatible with farm use or converted to a use incompatible with farm use by the owner, the owner is liable to pay an amount equal to the additional tax at the current mill levy together with 8 percent interest for the preceding seven years, as though the land had not been assessed for farm use purposes."

ARIZONA

Relevant Statutes:
Ariz. Rev. Stat. §42-12002 (1)(a) & (b); Ariz. Rev. Stat. §42-15002; Ariz. Rev. Stat. § 42-12151~ § 42-12153; Ariz. Rev. Stat. § 42-13101

Eligible Uses:
Agricultural/Farmland including land used in the processing of various specified commodities. County assessors are required to make an onsite inspection of 25 percent of the agricultural land in their county each year, so that all of these properties are visited and appraised within every four years. The most evident of the nonqualifying factors is the termination of the agricultural operation. But in many instances, the assessor must consider other factors to determine whether or not an agricultural property has changed use, including:
- A pending application for rezoning;
- A recorded subdivision plat, especially if the land is divided into lots of one acre or less;
- Recent installation of survey stakes or roads for nonagricultural development; and
- Installation of utility services.

Eligibility Requirements:
1. Property has been in active production according to generally accepted agricultural practices for at least three of the last five years.
2. There is a reasonable expectation of operating profit, exclusive of land cost, from the agricultural use of the property.
3. If the property consists of noncontiguous parcels, the noncontiguous parcels must be managed and operated on a unitary basis, and each parcel must make a functional contribution to the agricultural use of the property.

Method of UV Assessment:
Income approach only using capitalized average annual net cash rental of property. Net cash rental of property is average of net cash rental (excluding real estate and

(*continued*)

sales taxes) for five previous years. Capitalized at a rate of 1.5 percent higher than average long-term annual effective interest rate for all new Farm Credit Services loans for five previous years.

Development Penalty:
No. Penalties apply only for false information or failure to notify of change in use. Liable for full tax difference and 25 percent of additional tax as penalty.

ARKANSAS

Relevant Statutes:
Ark. Code § 26-26-407(b); Ark. Code § 26-26-407(f)~ § 26-26-407(i)

Eligible Uses:
Agricultural/Farmland; Forestland/Timber Production; Other Land Uses

Method of UV Assessment:
Agricultural land, pastureland, and timberland valuation shall be based on the productivity of the agricultural land, pastureland, or timberland soil. Eighteen soil quality categories are employed by the Assessment Coordination Department. Each year the Department shall develop and calculate capitalization rates by using appropriate long-term federal security rates, risk rates, management rates, and other appropriate financial rates. However, the capitalization rate shall not be less than 8 percent or more than 12 percent.

Recent Use Values ($ per acre):
There are four agricultural use value regions within the state. In the Delta region in 2013, cropland use values range from $135 to $790 per acre based on soil capability. See www.arkansas.gov/acd/pdfs/2012_AGRICULTURAL_REPORT.pdf for data from other regions and for timberland and pastureland.

Development Penalty:
Penalties apply, but only upon failure to report change in use. If any person shall fail to give written notice of a change in use of land, the person shall be subject to a penalty in an amount equal to three years of taxes on the land at the value in the new use or conversion use.

CALIFORNIA

Relevant Statutes:
Cal. Govt. Code. § 51200 ~ § 51207, Cal. Revenue and Taxation Code § 421, Cal. Revenue and Taxation Code § 423.5 ~ § 437

Eligible Uses:
Agricultural/Farmland; Conservation/Open Space; Forestland/Timber Production

Eligibility Requirements:
An agricultural preserve defines the boundary of an area within which a city or county will enter into contracts with landowners. The boundary is designated by

resolution of the board of supervisors or city council having jurisdiction. Only land located within an agricultural preserve is eligible for a Williamson Act contract. Preserves are regulated by rules and restrictions designated in the resolution to ensure that the land within the preserve is maintained for agricultural or open space use. An agricultural preserve must consist of no less than 100 acres.

Contract Length:
The Williamson Act creates an arrangement whereby private landowners contract with counties and cities to voluntarily restrict their land to agricultural and compatible open-space uses. The vehicle for these agreements is a rolling term 10-year contract (i.e., unless either party files a "notice of nonrenewal," the contract is automatically renewed for an additional year). Generally cancellation is impermissible within the first nine years of a ten-year contract, and in the last year the owner may decide not to renew the contract. If the owner meets the strict cancellation requirements, then the owner is liable for 12.5 percent and up to 25 percent of the fair market valuation of the property. In certain situations this penalty may be waived (e.g., land is required for public purpose). As of 2013, all counties except Del Norte, San Francisco, Inyo, and Yuba offer Williamson Act contracts.

Method of UV Assessment:
Varied methods: open space for wildlife—average current per-acre value based on recent sales including the sale of an undivided interest therein (Cal. Revenue and Taxation Code § 423.7); open space restricted for production of timber for commercial purposes—value of timber (Cal. Revenue and Taxation Code § 423.5); agricultural/farmland—based on actual or typically equivalent rent income (Cal. Revenue and Taxation Code § 423 (a)); discount rate provided by board "arithmetic mean, rounded to the nearest 1/4 percent, of the yield rate for long-term United States government bonds, as most recently published by the Federal Reserve Board as of September 1, and the corresponding yield rates for those bonds, as most recently published by the Federal Reserve Board as of each September 1 immediately prior to each of the four immediately preceding assessment years." (Cal. Revenue and Taxation Code § 423[b]) + other factors (such as risk component, component for property taxes, and component for amortization).

Development Penalty:
Yes. Cancellation fee equal to 12.5 percent (and up to 25 percent) of fair market valuation of property (Cal. Govt. Code. § 51283[b]).

COLORADO

Relevant Statutes:
Colo. Rev. Stat. § 39-1-102 ~ Colo. Rev. Stat. § 39-1-103; Colo. Rev. Stat. § 39-1-102 ~ Colo. Rev. Stat. § 39-1-103

Eligible Uses:
Agricultural/Farmland; Forestland/Timber Production

(continued)

Eligibility Requirements:
For property tax purposes, land must meet one of several requirements to qualify for agricultural classification, including the following:

1. A parcel of land that was used the previous two years and is presently used as a farm or a ranch, or is being restored through conservation practices. Such land must have been classified or eligible for classification as agricultural land during the 10 years preceding the year of assessment.
2. A parcel of land that has at least 40 acres of forestland and that is subject to a forest management plan.

Method of UV Assessment:
The actual value of agricultural land, exclusive of improvements, is based on the earning or productive capacity of the land. The landlord's gross income is calculated by multiplying the 10-year average price of the commodity or grazing rental rate by the yield associated with the subject property's soil classification, and then multiplying that figure by the typical landlord's crop share. The 10-year average of typical landlord expenses (statewide) is subtracted from the landlord's gross income to arrive at the landlord's net income. The net income is then capitalized by the statutory 13 percent rate to arrive at an indication of actual value. The assessed value of the land is calculated by multiplying the actual use value of the land by the assessment ratio (currently 29 percent).

Development Penalty:
No.

CONNECTICUT

Relevant Statutes:
Conn. Gen. Stat. § 203-12-63; Conn. Gen. Stat. § 203-12-107a ~ 203-12-107g; Conn. Gen. Stat. § 203-12-504 ~ 203-12-504h; Conn. Gen. Stat. § 203-12-96 ~ § 203-12-100

Eligible Uses:
Agricultural/Farmland; Forestland/Timber Production; Maritime Heritage Land; Open Space

Eligibility Requirements:
For forestland, not less than 25 acres; not exceeding in value of $100/acre; application for classification to state forester accompanied by description and other documents as requested.

Application and Renewal:
Application to town assessor with no annual renewal required.

Method of UV Assessment:
For farmland, capitalization of land rents obtained by surveys of landowners. Capitalization rate of 11.5 to 12.5 percent per year based on five-year rolling average of Federal Credit Service mortgage rate adjusted for tax rate and risk factor.

Recent Use Values:
Effective 2010, use values for tillable farmland range from $225 to $2,400 per acre. For forestland, the recommended use value is $130 per acre.

Development Penalty:
Yes. May be subject to a conveyance tax penalty, especially if it is within a 10-year period of the initial date of classification (10 percent if within one year, 9 percent if within two years, and so on).

DELAWARE

Relevant Statutes:
Del. Code tit. 9, § 8329 ~ § 8337

Eligible Uses:
Agricultural/Farmland; Forestland/Timber Production

Eligibility Requirements:
Land shall be deemed to be actively devoted to agricultural, horticultural, or forestry use when: (1) not less than 10 acres are in such use, and the gross sales of agricultural, horticultural, or forestry products produced thereon together with any agricultural program payments and sales of commodities received under government entitlement programs have averaged at least $1,000 per year within a two-year period of time immediately preceding the tax year in issue, or there is clear evidence of anticipated yearly gross sales and such payments amounting to at least $1,000 per year, within a two-year period of time; or (2) less than 10 acres are in such use and the gross sales of agricultural, horticultural, or forestry products produced thereon together with any agricultural program payments and sales of commodities received under government entitlement programs shall have averaged at least $10,000 per year within a two-year period of time immediately preceding the tax year in issue, or there is clear evidence of anticipated yearly gross sales and such payments amounting to at least $10,000 per year within a two-year period of time. In computing such anticipated yearly gross sales for land under 10 acres in such use, the maximum amount computed from future sales of forestry products shall be not more than $2,000 annually.

Application and Renewal:
Application shall be submitted by the owner to the assessor of the taxing district in which such land is situated on or before February 1 of the year immediately preceding the tax year for which such valuation, assessment, and taxation are sought; provided, however, that unless the eligibility of land under this section changes, those applications that have met the provisions to qualify under this chapter shall be automatically renewed without the owner having to apply annually.

Method of UV Assessment:
The assessor in valuing land that qualifies as land actively devoted to agricultural, horticultural, or forestry use under the tests prescribed by this section, and as to

(continued)

which the owner thereof has made timely application for valuation, assessment, and taxation under this section for the tax year in issue, shall consider only those indicia of value of such land as established by the State Farmland Evaluation Advisory Committee. The primary objective of the committee shall be the determination of the ranges in fair value of such land based on its productive capabilities when devoted to agricultural, horticultural, or forest uses. In making these annual determinations of value, the committee shall consider available evidence of agricultural, horticultural, or forest capability derived from the soil survey and such other evidence of value of land devoted exclusively to agricultural, horticultural, or forest uses as it may in its judgment deem pertinent.

Development Penalty:
Yes. Loss of eligibility can be triggered by a change in land use, rezoning, or approval of a site plan. Such land shall be subject to rollback taxes for the 10 previous tax years.

FLORIDA

Relevant Statutes:
Fla. Stat. § 193.461; Fla. Stat. § 193.011; Fla. Stat. § 193.501; Fla. Stat. § 193.011

Eligible Uses:
Agricultural/Farmland; Forestland/Timber Production; Conservation/Open Space; Parks/Recreation

Eligibility Requirements:
Florida law mandates that "only lands that are used primarily for bona fide agricultural purposes shall be classified agricultural." The term "bona fide agricultural purposes" means good-faith commercial agricultural use of the land; e.g., length of time, continuous use, purchase price paid, size, etc. Sale of land for a purchase price that is three or more times the agricultural assessment placed on the land shall create a presumption that such land is not used primarily for agricultural purposes. This presumption may be rebutted upon showing of special circumstances by the landowner. Lands under these programs that are converted to fallow uses, or are otherwise not producing income, shall continue to be classified as agricultural lands and shall be assessed at a de minimis value of no more than $50 per acre.

Application and Renewal:
Existing property owners with agricultural classification will receive an automatic renewal notice each year. If any changes to the land have occurred, it is the responsibility of the taxpayer to bring it to the property appraiser's attention.

Method of UV Assessment:
Factors taken into consideration include parcel size, condition, market value, income produced, productivity, merchantability of agricultural product, etc. A five-year moving average of data is to be used for income approach.

Recent Use Values ($ per acre):
For some agricultural land uses, the reduction in taxes for Greenbelt Classification versus market value may exceed 90 percent.

Development Penalty:
No.

GEORGIA

Relevant Statutes:
Ga. Code Ann. § 48-5-7; Ga. Code Ann. § 48-5-7.1; Ga. Code Ann. § 48-5-7.5

Eligible Uses:
Agricultural/Farmland; Forestland/Timber Production; Other Land Uses

Eligibility Requirements:
Maximum of 2,000 acres of a single person for good-faith production of agricultural products, timber, subsistence farming, or commercial production subject to qualifications; annual filing of inspection report. Qualifying property owners include individuals, naturalized citizens, and family-farm corporations.

Contract Length:
In making application for preferential assessment, qualifying taxpayers must sign a covenant (contract) agreeing to continuously maintain the property in agricultural pursuits for a period of 10 years. Transfers of ownership are allowed, provided the property is transferred to another qualifying entity that agrees to continue the property in agricultural pursuits for the remainder of the covenant period.

Method of UV Assessment:
There are several programs in Georgia. Preferential agricultural property is assessed at 30 percent of property's fair market value instead of the 40 percent otherwise required for real property. Conservation use valuation provides for the revenue commissioner to annually develop a table of current use values to be used in all counties. It is based on a legislated formula that takes into account the amount of income the land is capable of producing when growing certain crops and timber and factors found in market data using only farmer-to-farmer land sales. The data is grouped into nine agricultural districts in Georgia. Unlike the Preferential Agricultural Assessment Program, the valuation of property in conservation use covenants is most significant in urban areas of North Georgia.

Development Penalty:
Yes. In the Preferential Assessment Program, the penalty shall be computed by multiplying the amount by which the preferential assessment has reduced taxes otherwise due for the year in which the covenant breach occurs times: (1) a factor of five if the breach occurs in the first or second year of the covenant period; (2) a factor of four if the breach occurs during the third or fourth year of the covenant period; (3) a factor of three if the breach occurs during the fifth or sixth year of the covenant period;

(continued)

or (4) a factor of two if the breach occurs in the seventh, eighth, ninth, or tenth year of the covenant period. This penalty shall bear monthly interest at the rate specified in Code Section 48-2-40 from the date the covenant is breached. In the Conservation Use Valuation Program, the penalty is twice the tax savings from use-value assessment for one year + interest of 1 percent per month.

HAWAII

Relevant Statutes:
Haw. Rev. Stat. § 246-10; Maui Code of the County §3.48.350(A); Kauai County Code 1987 §5A-9.1; Hawaii County Code Chapter 19, art 8, §19-60

Eligible Uses:
Land Zoned for Agricultural Use; Forestland/Timber Production; Wasteland Development Land; Native Forest Land (Hawaii County); Golf Courses

Eligibility Requirements:
(Hawaii) land dedicated for commercial activity used on a continuous and regular basis for intensive agriculture, orchards, feed crops, and fast rotation forestry or pasture and slow rotation forestry with a minimum lot size per farm operation for the dedicated category; within zoned district (Kauai) evidence that land enjoys County Department of Water agricultural water rates, filed copies from the immediate preceding year of U.S. Internal Revenue Service Schedule F forms showing profit or loss from farming; filed copies of federal fuel tax exemptions claims made pursuant to Sec. 6427(c) of the U.S. Internal Revenue Code; sales receipts generated from the listed activities; a valid, current state general excise tax license; and covenants, conditions, and restrictions encumbering or affecting the property that prohibit or limit agricultural activities; other physical evidence such as grazing livestock, fences, etc.; other criteria for land areas part of tree farm management plan of over or under 100 acres (Maui) land dedicated must be used for the cultivation of crops such as sugarcane, pineapple, truck crops, orchard crops, ornamental crops, or the like, substantially and continuously.

Contract Length:
10- or 20-year dedication period

Method of UV Assessment:
Assessment of dedicated agricultural land at 50 percent of fair market value. Wasteland assessed at its value as wasteland for five years.

Development Penalty:
Yes.
Hawaii: Rollback tax—Difference of assessed tax and highest and best use; 10 percent penalty (of the higher tax); maximum of ten years. Deferred or rollback tax schedule: (1) Breach of the restrictions on use within five years of the dedication shall result in a rollback to the date of the dedication; (2) breach of the restrictions on use within six years of the dedication shall result in a rollback of four years from the date

of the breach; (3) breach of the restrictions on use within seven years of the dedication shall result in a rollback of three years from the date of the breach; and (4) breach of the restrictions on use within eight or nine years of the dedication shall result in a rollback of two years from the date of the breach.

Kauai and Maui: Dedication shall be canceled and special tax assessment privilege retroactive to the date of the dedication based on higher use shall be payable with a 10-percent-a-year penalty, not to exceed term of the original dedication.

IDAHO

Relevant Statutes:
Idaho Code Ann. § 63-602K; Idaho Code Ann. § 63-604; Idaho Code § 63-605; Idaho Admin. Code r. 35.01.03.614; Idaho Code Ann. § 63-1701 ~ § 63-1708; Idaho Admin. Rules 35.01.03.962; Idaho Admin. Rules 35.01.03.964

Eligible Uses:
Agricultural/Farmland; Conservation/Open Space; Other Land Uses

Eligibility Requirements:
For farmland, a total of more than 5 acres. If less than 5 acres, then land should agriculturally produce for sale or home consumption the equivalent of 15 percent or more of the owner's or lessee's AGI, or gross revenues of $1,000 or more. Until these requirements are shown for land less than 5 acres, land shall be presumed to be non-agricultural land. Land used to protect wildlife and wildlife habitat or land being managed pursuant to a conservation easement or a conservation agreement is eligible for tax status of land devoted to agriculture. For forestland, at least 5 acres but not more than 5,000 acres. Yield tax in lieu of and replacement for property taxes on timber. Yield tax rate shall be 3 percent of stumpage value as determined by the state tax commission (based on five-year rolling average value of comparable timber harvested from state timber sales within the stumpage value zone and/or the best available data for the same five-year period).

Method of UV Assessment:
Exemption of that portion of the value of agricultural land that represents the excess over the actual use value of such land established by comparable sales data compared to value established by capitalization of economic rent or long-term average crop rental at a capitalization rate that shall be the rate of interest charged by the Spokane office of the Farm Credit System averaged over the immediate past five years plus a component for the local tax rate.

Recent Use Values ($ per acre):
$51–$154 for forestland (2004).

Development Penalty:
Not for agricultural land. For forestland, a rollback penalty of up to 10 years.

(continued)

ILLINOIS

Relevant Statutes:
Ill. Comp. Stat. 35-§ 200/10-110 ~ § 200/10-147; Ill. Comp. Stat. 35-§200/10-500
~§200/10-520

Eligible Uses:
Agricultural/Farmland; Conservation/Open Space; Forestland/Timber Production

Eligibility Requirements:
A parcel of land used for agricultural purposes for at least two consecutive years is
eligible for a preferential assessment. More than 10 acres that promote conservation,
protect air or streams or water supplies, enhance natural or scenic resources, con-
serve landscaped areas, such as public or private golf courses, enhance value to public,
or preserve historic sites. Property under forest management plan accepted by Department of Natural Resources.

Method of UV Assessment:
Farmland is assessed based on its agricultural economic value (AEV) (i.e., its ability
to produce income) rather than on 33⅓ percent of its fair market value. The AEV is a
calculation based on an average of prices paid for agricultural products, production
costs, and interest rates over a five-year period. Assessing officials' value all farmland
in the county based on its productivity, taking into account the land's actual use,
slope, erosion, flooding, and other factors that affect productivity. For 2014, the capitalization rate applied to net farm income is 5.61 percent. Outside Cook County, eligible forestland to be valued at one-sixth of its AEV as cropland.

Recent Use Values:
For 2014, certified use values for agricultural land range from $15.26 to $645.93 per
acre.

Development Penalty:
No, for farmland and forestland. Yes, for open space land, a three-year rollback penalty with 5 percent interest.

INDIANA

Relevant Statutes:
Ind. Code § 6-1.1-4-4.5(e); Ind. Code § 6-1.1-4-13; Ind. Code § 6-1.1-6-1 ~§6-1.1-6-27;
Ind. Code §6-1.1-6.2-1~§6-1.1-6.2-27; Ind. Code § 6-1.1-6.7-1 ~§ 6-1.1-6.7-25

Eligible Uses:
Agricultural/Farmland; Forestland/Timber Production; Other Land Uses (Wind-
break, Water Filtration Strip, Native Forest Lands)

Eligibility Requirements:
IC 6-1.1-4-13(a) declares, "In assessing or reassessing land, the land shall be assessed
as agricultural land only when it is devoted to agricultural use." IC 6-1.1-4-12 states
that if land assessed on an acreage basis (i.e., agricultural land) is subdivided into

lots, or land is rezoned for, or put to, a different use, the land shall be reassessed on the basis of its new classification. If improvements are added to real property, the improvements shall be assessed.

Method of UV Assessment:

The Department of Local Government Finance shall give written notice to each county assessor of the USDA's soil survey data and the appropriate soil productivity factor for each type or classification of soil shown on the survey. This data is used in determining the true tax value of agricultural land. The value in use of agricultural land is calculated by dividing the net income of each acre by the appropriate capitalization rate. The net income of agricultural land can be based on either the net operating income or the net cash rent. Net operating income is the gross income received from the sale of crops less the variable costs (i.e., seed and fertilizer) and fixed costs (i.e., machinery, labor, property taxes) of producing crops. The net cash rent income is the gross cash rent of an acre of farmland less the property taxes on the acre. Both methods assume the net income will continue to be earned into perpetuity.

Recent Use Values:

The base rate for assessment year 2012/tax year 2013 is $1,630 per acre as set by the Department of Local Government Finance based on trending rents, yields, prices, and interest rates.

Development Penalty:

No, for enrolled farmland. Yes, for forestland and other land uses. All tax savings from use-value assessment up to period of 10 years + 10 percent interest + $100 for each withdrawal + $50 per acre for property enrolled after June 30, 2006.

IOWA

Relevant Statutes:

Iowa Code § 441.21(1)(e) ~ §441.21(1)(g); Iowa Admin. Code 701–71.1

Eligible Uses:

Agricultural/Farmland; Conservation/Open Space; Forestland/Timber Production; Other Land Uses

Eligibility Requirements:

Agricultural real estate shall include all tracts of land and the improvements and structures located on them that are in good faith used primarily for agricultural purposes, except buildings that are primarily used or intended for human habitation.

Method of UV Assessment:

The actual value of agricultural property shall be determined on the basis of productivity and net earning capacity of the property determined on the basis of its use for agricultural purposes capitalized at a rate of 7 percent and applied uniformly among counties and among classes of property. Any formula or method employed to deter-

(continued)

mine productivity and net earning capacity of property shall be adopted in full by rule. Use of five-year averages of county-level crop yields and farm prices.

Development Penalty:
No.

KANSAS

Relevant Statutes:
Kan. Stat. Ann. §79-503a; Kan. Stat. Ann. §79-1439(b)(1)(B); Kan. Stat. Ann. § 79-1476

Eligible Uses:
Agricultural/Farmland; Forestland/Timber Production

Eligibility Requirements:
Agricultural land is classified as dry cultivated land, irrigated land, tame grassland, and native grassland.

Method of UV Assessment:
The appraised value of agricultural land is based on the productive potential directly attributed to the natural capabilities of the land, not fair market value. Cultivated land is valued using an eight-year average of the landlord share of net income, with soil types used to recognize land productivity potential. For grassland, an eight-year average of the landlord share of the net rental income is used. In the case of grassland, productivity is established by use of the grazing index assigned to each soil type. The resulting eight-year average landlord net income is divided by a capitalization rate to arrive at the appraised value.

The following three components make up the capitalization rate:

1. The five-year average of the Federal Land Bank interest rate on new loans in Kansas as of July 1 of each year.
2. An "add on" of not less than .75 percent or more than 2.75 percent determined by the Director of Property Valuation.
3. As of property tax year 2003, the capitalization rate shall not be less than 11 percent or more than 12 percent as mandated by the 2002 Kansas Legislature.
4. The county average agricultural property tax rate. This accounts for property taxes on agricultural land as an expense.

The sum of these three components is the capitalization rate percentage that is divided into the landlord net income (LNI) to arrive at the agricultural value.

Development Penalty:
No.

KENTUCKY

Relevant Statutes:
Ky. Rev. Stat. Ann. § 132.010; Ky. Rev. Stat. Ann. § 132.450; Ky. Rev. Stat. Ann. § 132.454

Eligible Uses:
Agricultural/Farmland; Forestland/Timber Production; Other Land Uses

Eligibility Requirements:
At least ten acres used for the production of livestock, livestock products, poultry, poultry products, and/or the growing of tobacco and/or other crops including timber; or at least five acres commercially used for aquaculture; or any tract of land devoted to meeting the requirements and qualifications for payments pursuant to agricultural programs under an agreement with state or federal government.

Horticultural land must be at least five acres used for cultivation of a garden, orchard, or the raising of fruits or nuts, vegetables, flowers, or ornamental plants. Property rezoned at the owner's request to other than agricultural use qualifies for agricultural assessment until the land changes from agricultural use to the use granted under the new zoning classification. When land that has been valued and taxed as agricultural land for five or more consecutive years under the same ownership fails to qualify for the classification through no other action on the part of the owner or owners other than ceasing to farm the land, the land shall retain its agricultural classification for assessment and taxation purposes. Classification as agricultural land shall expire upon change of use by the owner or owners or upon conveyance of the property to a person other than a surviving spouse.

Method of UV Assessment:
Agricultural or horticultural value means the use value of agricultural or horticultural land based on income-producing capability and comparable sales of farmland purchased for farm purposes where the price is indicative of farm use value, excluding sales representing purchases for farm expansion, better accessibility, and other factors that inflate the purchase price beyond farm use value, if any.

Development Penalty:
No. Repayment of deferred tax is mentioned on some county websites (for up to two rollback years), but the statute section referred to (Ky. Rev. Stat. Ann. § 132.450(2)(f)) no longer exists.

LOUISIANA

Relevant Statutes:
La. Rev. Stat. Ann. § 3:4321; La. Rev. Stat. Ann. § 47.2301 ~ § 47.2307; La. Admin. Code tit. 61, § 301.

Eligible Uses:
Agricultural/Farmland; Forestland/Timber Production; Other Land Uses

(continued)

Eligibility Requirements:
In order to be classified as bona fide agricultural, horticultural, marsh, or timberland and assessed at its use value under the provisions of Article VII, Section 18(C), of the Louisiana Constitution of 1974, it must meet the definition of bona fide agricultural, horticultural, marsh, or timberland.

Bona fide agricultural land is land devoted to the production for sale, in reasonable commercial quantities, of plants and animals, or their products, useful to man, and agricultural land under a contract with a state or federal agency restricting its use for agricultural production. Bona fide horticultural land is land devoted to the production for sale, in reasonable commercial quantities, of fruits, vegetables, flowers or ornamental plants, and horticultural land under a contract with a state or federal agency restricting its use for horticultural production. Bona fide marshland is wetland other than bona fide agricultural, horticultural, or timberland. Bona fide timberland is land stocked by forest trees of any size and species, or formerly having such tree cover within the last three years and not currently developed or being used for nonforest purposes, and devoted to the production, in reasonable commercial quantities, of timber and timber products, and timberland under a contract with a state or federal agency restricting its use for timber productions. To qualify, a property must be a minimum of 3 acres or have produced an average gross annual income of at least $2,000 for 4 preceding years in one of the designated classifications.

Method of UV Assessment:
Use value equals net income in qualifying use divided by a capitalization rate. In applying this formula the assessors shall utilize the use-value table and the capitalization rate as determined by the Louisiana Tax Commission or its successor, and said formula shall be applied uniformly throughout the state. The Louisiana Tax Commission, or its successor, shall determine a capitalization rate for use in determining use value of agricultural and horticultural land by considering the following factors: (1) physical and economic risk; (2) effect of relative marketability of agricultural and horticultural lands on liquidity of investments; (3) competition with other investments and prevailing interest rate; and (4) any other appropriate factors. In no event shall the capitalization rate be less than 12 percent. In determining an appropriate capitalization rate for timberland to be used in the use-value table, the Louisiana Tax Commission or its successor shall take into consideration the following factors: (1) physical and economic risk; (2) effect of relative marketability of timberlands on liquidity of said investments; (3) competition with other investments and prevailing interest rates; and (4) any other factors that may be appropriate. In no event shall the capitalization rate be less than 10 percent.

Recent Use Values ($ per acre):
Assessed value of agricultural land in 2004 ranging from $12.40 to $34.79 per acre.

Development Penalty:
No penalty for change of use, but if the landowner obtains a use-value assessment by means of false certifications on his application, or fails to timely notify the assessor of loss of eligibility for use-value assessment, he shall be liable for a penalty equal to five times the difference between the tax under a market-value assessment and the tax under a use-value assessment for the tax years in which the use-value assessment was attributable to the false certifications or failure to timely notify the assessor of loss of eligibility.

MAINE

Relevant Statutes:
Me. Rev. Stat. Ann. tit. 36, § 1131 ~ § 1140(B); Me. Rev. Stat. Ann. tit. 36, § 571 ~ § 584A; Me. Rev. Stat. Ann. tit. 36, § 1101 ~ 36, § 1121

Eligible Uses:
Agricultural/Farmland; Forestland/Timber Production; Conservation/Open Space; Parks/Recreation; Working Waterfronts

Eligibility Requirements:
"Working waterfront land" means a parcel of land, or a portion thereof, abutting water to the head of tide or land located in the intertidal zone that is used primarily or used predominantly to provide access to or support the conduct of commercial fishing activities. Application by owner with annual recertification.

"Forestland" means land used primarily for growth of trees to be harvested for commercial use, but does not include ledge, marsh, open swamp, bog, water, and similar areas, which are unsuitable for growing a forest product or for harvesting for commercial use even though these areas may exist within forestlands. Application requires a minimum of 10 acres of forestland, a forest management and harvest plan updated every 10 years, and evidence of compliance with plan.

"Farmland" means any tract or tracts of land, including woodland and waste-land, of at least five contiguous acres on which farming or agricultural activities have contributed to a gross annual farming income of at least $2,000 per year from the sales value of agricultural products in one of the two or three of the five calendar years preceding the date of application for classification. The farming or agricultural activity and income derived from that activity may be achieved by either the owner or a lessee of the land.

"Open space land" means any area of land, including state wildlife and management areas, sanctuaries, and preserves, the preservation or restriction of the use of which provides a public benefit in any of the areas by conserving scenic resources, enhancing public recreation opportunities, promoting game management, or preserving wildlife or wildlife habitat.

Application and Renewal:
Annual filing is not necessary, but assessor may request the filing of a new application at any time.

(continued)

Method of UV Assessment:

Agricultural use values shall be based on such considerations as farmland rentals, farmer-to-farmer sales, soil types and quality, commodity values, topography, and after considering state-developed guidelines for agricultural valuation. The state tax assessor determines the use valuation per acre for each forest type by region each year. These valuations are adopted through rulemaking each year and are made public before April 1. The use value of open space land is the sale price that parcel would command in the marketplace if it were required to remain in the particular category of open space land for which it qualifies, adjusted by the certified ratio. These values may be based on such considerations as sales of land subject to permanent conservation restrictions, sales of land subject to enforceable deed restrictions, and other relevant factors.

Recent Use Values:

Suggested values of $400 per acre for cropland and $325 per acre for pastureland.

Development Penalty:

For farmland that no longer qualifies, the penalty shall be the taxes that would have been assessed upon the land for the past five years, less all taxes that were actually paid during those years, plus interest at the rate set annually by the municipality during those five years of classification. Change from farmland to open space or vice versa may not be penalized if parcel meets eligibility requirements of the new classification. For forestland that no longer qualifies, depending upon the length of time that the parcel has been enrolled, the penalty would be an amount between 20 and 30 percent of the difference between the tree growth value and the fair market value.

MARYLAND

Relevant Statutes:

Md. Code, Tax-Prop. § 8-209 ~ § 8-211; Md. Code, Tax-Prop. § 13-301 ~ § 13-308; Md. Ann. Code Prop Tax § 9-107; Md. Ann. Code Prop Tax § 8-209.1; Md. Code Ann. Tax-Property § 8-102; Md. Regs. Code 18.02.03.05

Eligible Uses:

Golf Courses; Forestland/Timber Production; Agricultural/Farmland; Conservation/ Open Space

Eligibility Requirements:

Parcels less than 3 acres not eligible (with exceptions) for agricultural use assessment. In determining if a parcel of land of less than 20 acres, or not zoned for agricultural use, is actively used, the Department may require the owner of the land to affirm, under oath, on a standard form provided by the Department that the farm or agricultural use of the land results in an average gross income of at least $2,500. Golf course minimum of 9 holes and 50 acres. Conservation property means land that is unimproved, not used for commercial purposes, and subject to certain perpetual conservation easements. The owner of at least five contiguous acres of forestland may make an agreement with the Department of Natural Resources to place the land in the program for a minimum of 15 years.

Method of UV Assessment:
Value ranges determined by the Department of Assessments and Taxation are reported in the Maryland Assessment Procedures Manual. Assessment of farmland shall be maintained at levels compatible with the continued use of the land for farming and not be affected adversely by neighboring land uses of a more intensive nature or as if subdivided. Agricultural use values shall be calculated by capitalizing farmland rental income. Thus, ranges of value will be established for the entire state. The value ranges determined will become part of the Department's Procedures Manual and will be periodically updated.

Recent Use Values:
As of 2009, agricultural use values ranged between $125 and $500 per acre.

Development Penalty:
Yes. For agricultural land, there is a transfer tax between 3 and 5 percent of sales price based on size and condition of the parcel. The transfer tax is reduced by 25 percent for each consecutive full taxable year for which property was taxed without use assessment before the transfer.

MASSACHUSETTS

Relevant Statutes:
Mass. Gen. Laws ch. 61 §§ 1-8; Mass. Gen. Laws ch. 61A § 1-24; Mass. Gen. Laws ch. 61B § 1~18

Eligible Uses:
Agricultural/Farmland; Forestland/Timber Production; Conservation/Open Space; Parks/Recreation

Eligibility Requirements:
For agricultural land, at least five acres actively farmed during previous two years and generating at least $500 of annual sales receipts. For forestland, at least ten acres with a ten-year forest management plan approved by state forester. For recreational land, at least five contiguous acres used for certain recreational purposes and open to the public or members of a nonprofit organization, or be maintained in a substantially natural, wild, or open condition.

Application and Renewal:
Annual renewal of recreational land and farmland enrollment required. New management plan required for enrolled forestland after ten years.

Method of UV Assessment:
The rate of tax applicable to agricultural or horticultural land or forestland shall be the rate determined to be applicable to commercial property under chapter 59. The

(continued)

value of recreational land is to be based on use and in no event is to exceed 25 percent of the land's fair cash value.

Recent Use Values:
Recommended 2014 use value for harvested cropland ranges from $144 to $963 per acre. Forty dollars per acre recommended for nonproductive land and $160 per acre for pastureland.

Development Penalty:
For agricultural land, recreational land, and forestland, a rollback tax for five years with 5 percent interest included. A conveyance tax as high as 10 percent if disqualifying use occurs during the first decade and if conveyance tax is larger than rollback tax.

MICHIGAN

Relevant Statutes:
Mich. Comp. Laws § 324.36101 ~ § 324.36117;Mich. Comp. Laws Ann. § 211.7jj[1]; Mich. Comp. Laws §§ 324.51101~51119

Eligibility Requirements:
The State of Michigan does not have UVA of qualified rural lands. It does, however, permit preferential property taxation under the Commercial Forest Property, Qualified Forest Property Exemption, and Qualified Agricultural Property Exemption Acts. Enrolled agricultural and forest properties are exempt from up to 18 mills of school operating millages. There is no reduction of the assessed values of these properties because of their rural features. There is no minimum parcel size or minimum agricultural income for the enrolled agricultural properties. Enrolled forest properties must be at least 20 contiguous acres covered at least 80 percent by productive forest and subject to a forest management plan.

Development Penalty:
When properties no longer qualify for agricultural or forest property exemptions, they are subject to a seven-year recapture tax to recover tax savings during the period of enrollment.

MINNESOTA

Relevant Statutes:
Minn. Stat. § 88.47 ~ §88.53; Minn. Stat. § 290C.01 ~ 290C.13; Minn. Stat. § 273.111 – 273.114; Minn. Stat. §273.13 subd. 23(d)

Eligible Uses:
Vacant Rural Land; Agricultural Land; Forestland; Open Space

Eligibility Requirements:
Enrollment of at least 10 acres of Class 2a agricultural land devoted to sale of agricultural products under the Green Acres Program. Enrollment of Class 2b vacant rural

land not in agricultural production but contiguous to Green Acres property in the Rural Preserve Program. Enrollment of at least 20 acres but no more than 1,920 acres of Class 2c land not suitable for agriculture and with registered forest management plan in Managed Forest Land Program.

Method of UV Assessment:
Under the Green Acres Program, use of sales data for tillable land in the state's "purest agricultural [land] market" as a benchmark value and comparison to sales data in counties influenced by development pressures. Values of individual properties adjusted by county assessor to account for differences in soil quality and location. Under the Rural Preserve Program, acres are to be assessed at a "value without regard to outside influences" or its "rural preserve value," which must not exceed the class 2a tilled value for that county. Under the Managed Forest Land Program, a reduced class rate of 0.65 percent is applied to taxable market value to derive tax capacity.

Development Penalty:
Under the Green Acres and Rural Preserve Programs, owners of parcels that no longer qualify pay a rollback tax equal to the tax savings of the current and two previous tax years. There is no rollback provision for land that is no longer eligible for the Managed Forest Land Program.

MISSISSIPPI

Relevant Statutes:
Miss. Code Ann. § 27-35-50 (4) (b); Miss. Code Ann. 27-35-4

Eligible Uses:
Agricultural/Farmland; Forestland/Timber Production

Eligibility Requirements:
Land used for commercial production of agricultural commodities

Method of UV Assessment:
Agricultural land, like other locally assessed real property, is assessed for property tax purposes at a specified percentage of its true value, according to current use (Miss Code Ann. Sec. 27-35-50). Forestland and agricultural land is assessed at 15 percent (Class II property). An appraisal of land used for agricultural purposes must take into account soil types, productivity, and other criteria set forth in the land appraisal manuals of the Mississippi State Tax Commission. The income approach to valuation must be used, with a capitalization rate of not less than 10 percent and a moving average of not more than 10 years.

Development Penalty:
No.

(*continued*)

MISSOURI

Relevant Statutes:
Mo. Rev. Stat. § 254.010 ~ § 254.300; Mo. Rev. Stat. § 137.015~ § 137.021; Mo. Code Regs. tit. 12 § 30-4.010

Eligible Uses:
Agricultural/Farmland; Horticultural Land; Forestland

Eligibility Requirements:
"Agricultural and horticultural property" includes all real property used for agricultural purposes and devoted primarily to the raising and harvesting of crops; to the feeding, breeding, and management of livestock, which shall include breeding, showing, and boarding of horses; to dairying; or to any other combination thereof; and buildings and structures customarily associated with farming, agricultural, and horticultural uses. It includes lands enrolled in federal conservation programs and the land of some privately owned airports.

Method of UV Assessment:
Agricultural land being actively farmed is assessed according to productive capability, with a specific value per acre assigned based on soil productivity guidelines set by the State Tax Commission. Missouri statutes state that vacant and unused land is to be assessed at 12 percent of market value.

Development Penalty:
No.

MONTANA

Relevant Statutes:
Mont. Code Ann. § 15-44-101 ~ § 15-44-105; Mont. Code Ann. §15-6-143; Admin. R. Mont. 42.20.701 ~ 42.20.750; Mont. Code Ann. § 15-7-201 ~ 212; Mont. Code Ann. § 15-6-133

Eligible Uses:
Forestland/Timber Production; Agricultural/Farmland

Eligibility Requirements:
For agricultural land, properties over 160 acres with certain exceptions for lands greater than 20 acres; over half of the owner's Montana annual gross income is derived from agricultural production; minimum of $1,500 in annual gross income from the raising of agricultural products. Eligible forestland consists of at least 15 contiguous acres in one ownership that is capable of producing timber that can be harvested in commercial quantity and is producing timber unless the trees have been removed through harvest or by natural disaster, including but not limited to fire. Forestland includes land: (1) that has not been converted to another use; and (2) on which the annual net wood production equals or exceeds 25 cubic feet an acre at the culmination of mean annual increment.

Method of UV Assessment:
For enrolled forestland, properties are assessed at 0.29 percent of their forest productivity value. Forest productivity value is determined by capitalizing the value of the mean annual net wood production at the culmination of mean annual increment plus other agriculture-related income, if any, less annualized expenses, including but not limited to the establishment, protection, maintenance, improvement, and management of the crop over the rotation period. The capitalization rate for land is composed of a discount rate plus an effective tax rate. Each valuation zone has a unique capitalization rate. A single, statewide discount rate is calculated for forestland that represents a five-year average interest rate. The annual rate is calculated by the Northwest Farm Credit Services in Spokane. An effective tax rate is calculated for each forest valuation zone. The valuation formula for agricultural land is found in 15-7-201, MCA, *Legislative intent-value of agricultural property.* This formula is: $V = I/R$, where V is the value of each type of agricultural land, I is the net income of each type of agricultural land, and R is the capitalization rate.

Development Penalty:
No.

NEBRASKA

Relevant Statutes:
Neb. Rev. Stat. § 77-1343 ~ § 77-1347.01; Neb. Rev. Stat. § 77-1359; Neb. Rev. Stat. § 77-1371; Neb. Rev. Stat. § 77-1374 ~ 77; Neb. Rev. Stat. § 77-201; 1972 Constitutional Amendment

Eligible Uses:
Agricultural/Farmland

Eligibility Requirements:
Land is located outside the corporate boundaries of any sanitary and improvement district, city, or village except when subject to a conservation easement.

Method of UV Assessment:
The assessor shall capitalize net cash rent to determine a valuation based on the earnings of the property from the agricultural or horticultural use only in eight soil and climate areas. The valuation indicated by such an income capitalization approach shall be used as the special valuation if the market comparison approach results in a value that reflects a value influenced by purposes and uses other than agriculture or horticulture. The capitalization rate shall include, but not be limited to, an appropriate discount rate for the land use of the parcel of land, an adjustment for change in land value, and the effective tax rate for the parcel of land.

Development Penalty:
No.

(*continued*)

NEVADA

Relevant Statutes:
Nv. Rev. Stat. §361A.040 ~ Nv. Rev. Stat. §361A.090; Nv. Rev. Stat. §361A.170 ~ Nv. Rev. Stat. §361A.250; Nev. Rev. Stat.§361A.020~ §361A.090; Nev. Rev. Stat. § 361A.100; Nev. Rev. Stat. § 361A.160; Nev. Admin. Code § 361A.180

Eligible Uses:
Conservation/Open Space; Agricultural/Farmland; Forestland/Timber Production; Golf Courses

Eligibility Requirements:
Land located within classified area to promote conservation of open space and protection of other natural and scenic resources from unreasonable impairment, devoted exclusively to open-space use; or land used as golf course. At least 20 acres used for agricultural purposes.

Method of UV Assessment:
Open-space values equal taxable value of the open-space property times a factor of 0.74. The assessed value equals 35 percent of the open-space use value. For agricultural land, a five-year weighted average of net operating income may be capitalized into a measure of the value of the land per acre by multiplying the yield per acre, measured in tons per acre, by the net income per ton and then dividing the result by the capitalization rate. Capitalization rates typically vary between 8 and 12 percent, depending on the region and the type of land being valued. The result must be multiplied by the level of assessment for this property class (35 percent) to obtain an assessed value per acre.

Recent Use Values:
During 2010–2011, use values for cultivated land ranged from $68 to $175 per acre. For pastureland, the range was from $7 to $44 per acre.

Development Penalty:
Yes. For properties no longer eligible for UVA, a rollback tax equal to the tax savings of the current and six previous tax years is imposed. An additional penalty equal to 20 percent of the total accumulated deferred tax is assessed if owner fails to provide the written notice required upon change in use of parcel.

NEW HAMPSHIRE

Relevant Statutes:
N.H. Rev. Stat. Ann. § 79-A:1~79-A:26; N.H. Rev. Stat. Ann. § 79-A:1~79-A:26; N.H. Rev. Stat. Ann. §79:1~ 79:31; N.H. CUB 301.01~310.01

Eligible Uses:
Agricultural/Farmland; Forestland/Timber Production; Unproductive Land or Wetland

Eligibility Requirements:
Parcel must be at least 10 acres or provide $2,500 in annual agricultural or horticultural products.

Method of UV Assessment:
Farmland use values are based on a soil potential index. Forestland use values are based on: (1) grade severity of the terrain; (2) location—factors affecting accessibility of the forest products; and (3) site quality—ability of the site to grow trees. An additional 20 percent reduction in assessment is allowed for allowing certain public recreational uses of private land.

Recent Use Values:
For 2013–2014, use values for farmland range from $25 to $425 per acre. For white pine forest with documented stewardship, the range is $87 to $131 per acre. For unproductive land and wetland, the use value is $10 per acre.

Development Penalty:
A 10 percent land-use change tax is assessed based on current market value at the time the enrolled parcel changes to a nonqualifying use.

NEW JERSEY

Relevant Statutes:
N.J. Rev. Stat. § 54:4-23; N.J. Rev. Stat. § 54:4-23.2; N.J. Rev. Stat. § 54:4-23.5; N.J. Rev. Stat. § 54:4-23.8

Eligible Uses:
Agricultural/Farmland; Forestland/Timber Production; Other Land Uses

Eligibility Requirements:
Land must be devoted to agricultural and/or horticultural uses for at least two years prior to the tax year when application is made. Land must consist of at least five contiguous (adjoining) acres being farmed and/or under a woodlot management plan. Gross sales of products from the land must average at least $1,000 per year for the first five acres, plus an average of $5 per acre for each acre over five, except in the case of woodland or wetland where the income requirement is $.50 per acre for any acreage over five; or there is clear evidence of anticipated yearly gross sales, payments, or fees within a reasonable period of time dependent on the agricultural or horticultural products being produced. The applicant, on request of the assessor, at any time, must furnish proof of all the prerequisites necessary to show the land is eligible for Farmland Assessment, such as ownership, description, area, uses, gross sales, and income or fees from the agricultural or horticultural use of the land. By law, an on-site inspection of the land will be made by the tax assessor at least once every three years to verify eligibility.

Method of UV Assessment:
In 2012, 79 percent of net farm income was allocated to cropland harvested or pastured. This return to agricultural land was then capitalized using a rate of 10 percent

(continued)

that reflects the farm mortgage rate and a return to farm management and unpaid family labor.

Recent Use Values:

The annual report of the State Farmland Evaluation Advisory Committee reports county-level use values for six agricultural uses (including woodlands) and five soil quality groups.

Development Penalty:

Any parcel no longer eligible under the Farmland Assessment Act is subject to a roll-back tax equal to tax savings for the year in which eligibility is lost and the two years immediately prior.

NEW MEXICO

Relevant Statutes:

N.M. Stat. § 7-36-20; N.M. Admin. Code § 3.6.5.27

Eligible Uses:

Agricultural/Farmland; Forestland/Timber Production

Eligibility Requirements:

Agricultural use generally means the use of land for the production of plants, crops, trees, forest products, orchard crops, livestock, poultry, or fish. The term also includes the use of land that meets the requirements for payment of other compensation pursuant to a soil conservation program under an agreement with an agency of the federal government. Grazing valuation claims require proof of the presence of livestock. This may be in the form of a grazing lease, a personal property declaration of livestock that graze on the land, or some other proof of grazing use. One acre of nonimproved land is the minimum acreage that can be used as agriculture. If used for livestock grazing, the parcel must have the minimum number of acres capable of sustaining one animal unit.

Method of UV Assessment:

The production capacity of agricultural land shall be determined by the income method of valuation based on the income derived or capable of being derived from the use of the land for agricultural purposes. In setting the capitalization rate, consideration is given to the current interest rates for government loans, federal land bank loans, and production credit association loans.

Development Penalty:

No.

NEW YORK

Relevant Statutes:

N.Y. R.P.T (Real Property Tax) Law § 480-a; N.Y. R.P.T Law § 483-a; N.Y. A.G.M. Law § 301 ~ § 306

Eligible Uses:
Forestland/Timber Production; Agricultural/Farmland

Eligibility Requirements:
Agricultural land generally must consist of seven or more acres that were used in the preceding two years for the production for sale of crops, livestock, or livestock products. Land used in agricultural production includes cropland, pasture, orchards, vineyards, sugarbush, and crop acreage either set aside or retired under federal supply management or soil conservation programs. Up to 50 acres of farm woodland is eligible for an agricultural assessment per eligible tax parcel. Land and water used for aquacultural production are eligible. The annual gross sales of agricultural products generally must average $10,000 or more for the preceding two years. If an agricultural enterprise is less than seven acres, it may qualify if average annual gross sales equal $50,000 or more. Land located outside of an established agricultural district that receives an agricultural assessment is required to remain in agricultural use for eight years (land within an agricultural district is encumbered for five years) or be subject to a payment for conversion to nonagricultural use.

Method of UV Assessment:
The base agricultural assessment value is calculated as the average capitalized value of production per acre for the eight-year period ending in the second year preceding the year for which the agricultural assessment values are certified. In no event shall the change in the base agricultural assessment value for any given year exceed 10 percent of the base value of the preceding year.

Recent Use Values:
In 2013, agricultural use values ranged from $50 to $999 per acre depending on the parcel's mineral soil group. Farm woodland was assessed at $370 per acre.

Development Penalty:
A payment for conversion will be equal to five times the taxes saved in the most recent year that the land received an agricultural assessment. In addition, interest of 6 percent per year compounded annually will be added to the payment amount for each year that the land received an agricultural assessment, not exceeding five years. When only a portion of a parcel is converted, the assessor apportions the assessment and the agricultural assessment and determines the tax savings attributable to the converted portion.

NORTH DAKOTA

Relevant Statutes:
N.D. Cent. Code § 57-02-27.2

Eligible Uses:
Agricultural/Farmland

(continued)

Eligibility Requirements:
Agricultural land is land used to grow crops or graze livestock or for a greenhouse nursery operation. Property platted on or after March 30, 1981, is not agricultural property when any four of the following conditions exist: (1) The land is platted by the owner; (2) public improvements, including sewer, water, or streets, are in place; (3) topsoil is removed or topography is disturbed to the extent that the property cannot be used to raise crops or graze farm animals; (4) property is zoned other than agricultural; (5) property has assumed an urban atmosphere because of adjacent residential or commercial development on three or more sides; (6) the parcel is less than 10 acres [4.05 hectares] and not contiguous to agricultural property; or (7) the property sells for more than four times the county average true and full agricultural value.

Method of UV Assessment:
Agricultural value is defined as the "capitalized average annual gross return," except for inundated agricultural land. The "annual gross return" must be determined from crop share rent, cash rent, or a combination thereof reduced by estimated property taxes and crop marketing expenses incurred by farmland owners renting their lands on a cash or crop share basis. To find the "capitalized average annual gross return," the average annual gross return must be capitalized by a rate that is a 10-year average of the gross agribank mortgage rate of interest for North Dakota, but the rate used for capitalization may not be less than 8 percent for taxable year 2009, 7.7 percent for taxable year 2010, and 7 and 7.4 percent for taxable year 2011.

Recent Use Values:
The average estimated agricultural value per acre of agricultural lands in the state for the year 2013 was $496.59. This agricultural value ranged, by county, from $1,057 to $170 per acre. In 2011, property tax payments on agricultural land averaged $4.35 per acre statewide.

Development Penalty:
No.

NORTH CAROLINA

Relevant Statutes:
N.C. Gen. Stat.§§ 105-277.2 ~ 277.7; N.C. Gen. Stat. §§ 105-277.14~277.15; N.C. Gen. Stat. §§ 105-277.1F

Eligible Uses:
Agricultural/Farmland; Horticultural Land; Wildlife Conservation Land; Forestland/Timber Production

Eligibility Requirements:
Three land uses qualify under the Present Use Value Program:

Agricultural land—Land that is a part of a farm unit that is actively engaged in the commercial production or growing of crops, plants, or animals under a sound management program; minimum five acres; three years preceding average gross income of at least $1,000. Forestland—Land that is a part of a forest unit that is actively engaged in the commercial growing of trees under a sound management program; minimum 20 acres. Horticultural land—Land that is a part of a horticultural unit that is actively engaged in the commercial production or growing of fruits or vegetables or nursery or floral products under a sound management program; minimum five acres; average gross income of at least $1,000.

Beginning with the 2010 tax year, a new program for the taxation of wildlife conservation land went into effect. The land must be managed under a written wildlife habitat conservation agreement with the North Carolina Wildlife Resources Commission. The parcel must be at least 20 acres but no more than 100 acres. The land must have been owned by the qualifying owner for the previous five years (with certain exceptions).

Method of UV Assessment:
The Use-Value Advisory Board is established under the supervision of the Agricultural Extension Service of North Carolina State University. The Board must annually submit to the Department of Revenue a recommended use-value manual that contains the estimated cash rental rates for various land classifications, recommended net income ranges for forestland, capitalization rates, value per acre adopted by the Board for the best agricultural land not to exceed $1,200, and other recommendations. The capitalization rate for forestland shall be 9 percent. The capitalization rate for agricultural land and horticultural land must be no less than 6 percent and no more than 7 percent.

Development Penalty:
The difference between the market value and the present-use value is maintained in the tax assessment records as deferred taxes. When land becomes disqualified from the present use-value program, the deferred taxes for the current year and the three previous years with accrued interest will usually become due and payable.

OHIO

Relevant Statutes:
Ohio Rev. Code § 5713.30 ~ 5713.38; Ohio Admin. Code 5703:25-33

Eligible Uses:
Agricultural/Farmland; Conservation/Open Space; Forestland/Timber Production

Eligibility Requirements:
To qualify for the Current Agricultural Use Value (CAUV) Program, land must meet one of the following requirements during the three years preceding an application for enrollment: Ten or more acres must be devoted exclusively to commercial agricultural use or, if less than ten acres are devoted exclusively to commercial agricultural use, the farm must produce an average yearly gross income of at least $2,500. Agricultural use includes dairy farms, livestock operations, nursery stock, ornamental

(*continued*)

trees, sod, fish, beekeeping, or exotic animals. Commercial forestland of 10 or more acres may enroll in CAUV or Forest Tax Program. Noncommercial forestland adjacent to agricultural land may qualify for current use under certain circumstances.

Method of UV Assessment:
Each year, the Ohio Department of Taxation sets current agricultural use values for each of Ohio's soil types. These values are calculated from the capitalization of net income from agricultural products, assuming typical management, cropping and land use patterns, and crop yields. Crop prices and production costs are five-year weighted averages after discarding the highest and lowest prices of the past seven years. The 2013 capitalization rate including the average property tax rate is 6.7 percent. This cap rate is based on a five-year average of the Farm Credit Service interest rate and the assumption of a 60/40 loan/equity ratio for the farm operation.

Recent Use Values:
The 2013 CAUV per acre ranges from $350 to $3,780, depending on soil productivity type.

Development Penalty:
Yes. When land valued according to its agricultural use is converted to a different use, a charge is assessed on the land in an amount equal to the difference in the amount of tax levied on the converted land during the three tax years immediately preceding the year in which the conversion occurs.

OKLAHOMA

Relevant Statutes:
Okla. Stat. tit. 68 § 2817

Eligible Uses:
Agricultural/Farmland; Forestland/Timber Production; Conservation/Open Space

Eligibility Requirements:
Agricultural use includes production of crops, livestock, poultry, or cover crops. It also can include leaving the land idle for a government program (CRP) or for normal crop or livestock rotation. Land used for raising certain exotic animals to produce human food or other items of commercial value on agricultural land qualifies also. Using land for wildlife management is an agricultural use. Conservation buffer strips can also qualify and include any of the following approved Natural Resources Conservation Service (NRCS) practices that meet the standards and specifications of the NRCS:

1. alley cropping;
2. filter strip;
3. field border;
4. contour buffer strips;
5. grassed waterway;
6. riparian forest buffer; or
7. riparian herbaceous cover.

In order to qualify, the landowner must be participating in an Oklahoma Conservation Commission state cost-share program or federal conservation cost-share programs through the U.S. Department of Agriculture.

Method of UV Assessment:
The use value of agricultural land is based on the income capitalization approach using cash rent. A capitalization rate to be determined annually by the Ad Valorem Division of the Tax Commission is based on the sum of the average first mortgage interest rate charged by the Federal Land Bank for the immediately preceding five years, weighted with the prevailing rate or rates for additional loans or equity, and the effective tax rate.

Development Penalty:
No.

OREGON

Relevant Statutes:
Or. Rev. Stat. § 308A.300 ~ § 308A.330; Or. Rev. Stat. §308A.400 ~ §308A.430; Or. Rev. Stat. § 308A.450 ~ § 308A.703; Or. Rev. Stat. § 321.201~§321.222; Or. Rev. Stat. § 321.257~§321.390; Or. Rev. Stat. §321.805~321.855; Or. Rev. Stat. §308A.253.

Eligible Uses:
Conservation/Open Space; Parks/Recreation; Agricultural/Farmland; Forestland/Timber Production

Eligibility Requirements:
If land is in an Exclusive Farm Use (EFU) zone and is used primarily to make a profit in farming, it qualifies for special farm-use assessment. To qualify, the land must currently be used and have been used in the previous year exclusively for farm use. If land is not in an EFU zone but is used as farmland, it may receive the same assessment given to all qualifying EFU farmland. To qualify, the land must be currently used and have been used exclusively for farm use for the two previous years, and it must meet an income requirement in three of the five previous years. If the land is six and one-half acres or less, gross income from the farm use must be at least $650. If the land is more than six and one-half but fewer than thirty acres, gross income from the farm use must be $100 times the number of acres. If the land is thirty or more acres, gross income from the farm must be at least $3,000. The Department of Revenue by rule shall develop valuation models to be used to value forestland in western Oregon and eastern Oregon. The valuation models consider forestland sales, stumpage values, immediate harvest values, log prices, or other commercially reasonable factors or data that promote real market value analysis of forestland.

Method of UV Assessment:
Farm-use value for each land class is determined using an income method. Using this approach, the assessor must determine the capitalization rate and the net income per acre of farmland. The net income is the typical gross annual return

(*continued*)

(farmland rent), minus typical expenses. The capitalization rate is the five-year average Farm Credit Services mortgage rate plus the local property tax rate.

Development Penalty:
Yes. A rollback tax of up to ten years of tax savings is assessed on land in EFU zones. If the land is located within an urban growth boundary or is not in an EFU zone, the maximum number of rollback years is five.

PENNSYLVANIA

Relevant Statutes:
72 P.S. § 5490.1 ~ § 5490.13; 7 Pa. Code § 137b.1 ~ § 137b.133

Eligible Uses:
Agricultural/Farmland; Conservation/Open Space; Forestland/Timber Production.

Eligibility Requirements:
Three categories of private land can be placed in the Act 319 (Clean and Green) Program:
1. Agricultural Use—Land used for the purpose of producing an agricultural commodity or that is devoted to and meets the requirements and qualifications for payments or other compensation pursuant to a soil conservation program under an agreement with an agency of the federal government.
2. Agricultural Reserve—Noncommercial open-space lands used for outdoor recreation or the enjoyment of scenic or natural beauty and open to the public for such use, without charge or fee, on a nondiscriminatory basis.
3. Forest Reserve—Land stocked by forest trees of any size and capable of producing timber or other wood products.

The property must have at least 10 acres. Otherwise, if the property owner has less than 10 acres but can verify that the land is now devoted to agricultural use and has generated $2,000 annual gross income from agricultural commodities for the past three years, then the application may be considered.

Method of UV Assessment:
The Department of Agriculture supplies county assessment offices with county-specific use values annually. The county has the option of implementing these values, or using lower values. Agricultural use and agricultural reserve values are based on the income approach for land appraisal. The formula takes into consideration the state crop profit margin percentage for corn production, an average value of crop receipts per acre by county, a Soil Index Factor, and an average capitalization rate. Forest reserve values are based on the average value of timber in a particular county, or the average value of six timber types by county. The Pennsylvania Department of Conservation and Natural Resources calculates this value annually.

Development Penalty:
Yes. A rollback penalty is charged for the most recent seven years of program enrollment. A 6 percent simple interest charge will be imposed on the rollback tax amount.

RHODE ISLAND

Relevant Statutes:
R.I. Gen. Laws § 44-5-12(2); R.I. Gen. Laws § 44-27-1 ~ § 44-27-5; R.I. Gen. Laws § 44-27-9; R.I. Gen. Laws § 44-5-39

Eligible Uses:
Forestland/Timber Production; Agricultural/Farmland; Conservation/Open Space

Eligibility Requirements:
Farmland is land owned by a farmer, including woodland and wetlands, at least five acres of which are actively devoted to agricultural and horticultural use and which have produced a gross income from the sale of farm products of at least $2,500 in one of the last two years. The property must either have (or have applied for) a written conservation plan outlining best management practices recommended by the USDA and approved by the Department of Environmental Management. To be eligible for forestland classification the parcel must be 10 acres or more bearing a dense growth of trees, including young regenerating forest, which has been established either through natural regeneration or planting. The forest must be actively managed in accordance with the provisions of a written forest stewardship plan for the purpose of enhancing forest resources. The plan must be prepared by a qualified forester in consultation with the landowner. Open space is defined as undeveloped land (including farm or forestland) in tracts of 10 acres or larger (excluding the house site) where undeveloped land serves to enhance agricultural values, or land in its natural state that conserves forests, enhances wildlife habitat, or protects ecosystem health. Open space must be designated as open space in the Comprehensive Community Plan of the locality.

Application and Renewal:
For continued eligibility, the property owner must submit a certificate to the tax assessor each year confirming the land is still in agricultural use or conservation/open space.

Method of UV Assessment:
"In assessing real estate, which is classified as farmland, forest, or open space land . . . the assessors shall consider no factors in determining the full and fair cash value of the real estate other than those that relate to that use without regard to neighborhood land use of a more intensive nature."

Recent Use Values:
In 2006, agricultural use values ranged from $300 to $1,955 per acre. Forest-use values were $115 per acre. Open-space use values ranged from 10 to 30 percent of fair market value, depending on soil quality.

Development Penalty:
Yes. When property classified as farm-, forest-, or open-space land is withdrawn from the program, it is subject to a land use change tax. This tax is 10 percent of fair market value during the first six years of classification. This tax rate decreases one percentage point per year until the sixteenth year when the land use change tax is no longer

(continued)

due. Land classified as farmland, where the land has been farmed for five years prior to classification, is liable for a land use change tax of 10 percent of fair market value if the use is changed or classification is withdrawn during the first year of classification, and decreasing one percentage point per year until the tenth year.

SOUTH CAROLINA

Relevant Statutes:
S.C. Code Ann. § 12-43-220; S.C. Code Ann. § 12-43-233

Eligible Uses:
Agricultural/Farmland; Forestland/Timber Production

Eligibility Requirements:
State law provides six nonexclusive factors to be considered by county assessors in determining whether the tract in question is bona fide agricultural real property: (1) the nature of the terrain; (2) the density of the marketable product (timber, etc.) on the land; (3) the past usage of the land; (4) the economic merchantability of the agricultural product; (5) the use or not of recognized care, cultivation, harvesting, and like practices applicable to the product involved, and any implemented plans thereof; and (6) the business or occupation of the landowner or lessee, provided that purchase for investment purposes does not disqualify a tract if it is actually used for agricultural purposes. If the tract is used to grow timber, the tract must be five acres or more. Tracts of timberland of fewer than five acres qualify if they are contiguous to, or are under the same management system as, a tract of timberland that meets the minimum acreage requirement. Tracts of timberland of fewer than five acres are eligible to be agricultural real property if they are owned in combination with other tracts of agricultural real property that are not timberlands, but qualify as agricultural real property.

Method of UV Assessment:
SC Code §12-43-220(d)(2)(A) defines "fair market value for agricultural purposes" as the productive earning power based on soil capability to be determined by capitalization of typical cash rents or typical net income from timber and nontimber crops. After average net annual earnings have been established for agricultural lands, they must be capitalized based on a capitalization rate that includes:
1. an interest component (the interest rate component is the average coupon (interest) rate applicable on all bonds of the Federal Land Bank of Columbia, which serves South Carolina farmers, outstanding on July 1 of the crop-years being used to estimate net earnings and agricultural use-value);
2. a local property tax differential component;
3. a risk component; and
4. an illiquidity component.

Development Penalty:
Yes. If the property no longer qualifies for use-value assessment, the owner is liable for a rollback penalty for the current tax year (the year of change in use) and each of the immediately preceding five tax years.

SOUTH DAKOTA

Relevant Statutes:
S.D. Codified Laws § 10-6-31 ~ § 10-6-33; S.D. Codified Laws § 10-11-56; S.D. Codified Laws §10-12-42

Eligible Uses:
Agricultural/Farmland; Forestland/Timber Production

Eligibility Requirements:
Agricultural property includes all property and land used exclusively for agricultural purposes, both tilled and untilled, and the improvements on the land. A minimum of 20 acres of unplatted land or 80 acres of platted land (may be increased by the county to 160 acres) is eligible. At least one-third of the total family gross income of the owner is derived from the pursuit of agriculture.

Method of UV Assessment:
Beginning with the 2010 assessments (for taxes payable in 2011), agricultural land in South Dakota is assessed based on its productivity value. The productivity value formula multiplies the gross revenue by the landlord share percentages, and then divides this amount by the capitalization rate: [gross revenue × landlord share percentage] ÷ [cap rate]. The gross revenue for cropland is determined by using an eight-year Olympic average of yields and commodity prices. The gross revenue for noncropland is determined by using an eight-year Olympic average of cash rents. The landlord share percentages are 35 percent for cropland and 100 percent for noncropland. The capitalization rate is 6.6 percent. *Average Value of county*

Development Penalty:
No.

TENNESSEE

Relevant Statutes:
Tenn. Code Ann. § 67-5-1001 ~ § 67-5-1009

Eligible Uses:
Agricultural/Farmland; Conservation/Open Space; Forestland/Timber Production

Eligibility Requirements:
There are three types of land that may qualify for Greenbelt Program classification: farm, forestry, and open-space land. Agricultural land is land that "constitutes a farm unit engaged in the production or growing of crops, plants, animals, nursery, or floral products." The assessor may presume that land is used for agricultural purposes if it produces gross agricultural income (includes farm sales, farm rent, or federal farm support payments) averaging at least $1,500 per year over any three-year period in which the land is so classified. Property may also qualify if the owner or a parent or spouse has farmed the property for at least 25 years. Forestland does not

(continued)

have to produce a specific income to be considered for the Greenbelt Program. A forest management plan is required to maintain a forest classification. Open-space land is property maintained in an open or natural condition, preservation of which benefits the public by providing a natural setting for people. Although the property may be used for recreation, properties that have been significantly developed for this purpose, such as golf courses, do not qualify. The property must be included within a plan for preservation approved by state or local planning agencies, or the owner must execute a perpetual open-space easement. A minimum of 15 acres is required for farm and forestry properties and at least three acres for open-space land. There is a maximum of 1,500 acres per owner per county eligible for program enrollment.

Method of UV Assessment:
The Tennessee Division of Property Assessments is responsible for supplying the estimated annual agricultural income per acre for varying parcels of land in each county and for each of 12 different classes of land. Estimated income figures reflect consideration of soil productivity, crop prices, topography, flooding potential, rental value, and other factors. The capitalization rate applied to the estimated income stream is calculated by dividing the farm real estate interest expense by total farm real estate debt, as published by the Tennessee Agricultural Statistics Service. The capitalization rate used in calculations for 2006 was 6.77 percent.

Development Penalty:
Yes. Rollback taxes apply. The rollback period is three years for agricultural and forestland, five years for open-space land, and ten years for land under an open-space easement. Rollback taxes are a first lien against the disqualified property until paid.

TEXAS

Relevant Statutes:
Tex. Tax Code § 23.81 ~ § 23.87; Tex. Tax Code § 33.01; Tex. Tax Code § 23.41 ~ 46; Tex. Tax Code §23.51~23.57; Tex. Tax Code § 23.71 ~ § 23.79

Eligible Uses:
Agricultural/Farmland; Conservation/Open Space; Parks/Recreation; Forestland/ Timber Production

Eligibility Requirements:
"Recreational, park, or scenic use" means use for individual or group sporting activities, for park or camping activities, for development of historical, archaeological, or scientific sites, or for the conservation and preservation of scenic areas. Filing of deed instrument with county clerk; minimum five acres; minimum 10-year commitment. For agricultural use value, the property must have been exclusively devoted to agriculture for the three preceding years. The owner tends to land for agriculture as the primary occupation and primary source of income. Agricultural-use land cannot have a home equity loan.

Land qualifies for appraisal as forest-use land if it is currently and actively devoted principally to production of timber or forest products to the degree of intensity generally accepted in the area with intent to produce income and has been devoted principally to production of timber or forest products or to agricultural use that would qualify the land for appraisal for five of the preceding seven years.

Method of UV Assessment:

"Net to land" means the average annual net income derived from the use of open-space land that would have been earned from the land during the five-year period preceding the year before the appraisal by an owner using ordinary prudence in the management of the land and the farm crops or livestock produced or supported on the land and, in addition, any income received from hunting or recreational leases. The chief appraiser shall calculate net to land by considering the income that would be due to the owner of the land under cash lease, share lease, or whatever lease arrangement is typical in that area for that category of land, and all expenses directly attributable to the agricultural use of the land by the owner shall be subtracted from this owner income and the results shall be used in income capitalization. The capitalization rate to be used in determining the appraised value of qualified open-space land as provided by this subchapter is 10 percent or the interest rate specified by the Farm Credit Bank of Texas or its successor on December 31 of the preceding year plus 2½ percentage points, whichever percentage is greater.

Development Penalty:

Yes. For agricultural land, a rollback penalty consisting of additional taxes for the three years preceding the year in which the land is sold or diverted plus interest (6 to 12 percent). For recreational and park land and for open-space land, a rollback penalty equal to the difference in the amount of tax imposed and the amount that would have been imposed for that year plus interest of 7 percent for up to five previous years. For forestland, the difference in the amount of tax imposed and the amount that would have been imposed for that year plus interest of 7 percent.

UTAH

Relevant Statutes:

Utah Code § 59-2-501 ~ § 59-2-515; Utah Admin. Code r. 884-24-42; Utah Admin. Code r. 884-24-53

Eligible Uses:

Agricultural/Farmland; Forestland/Timber Production

Eligibility Requirements:

Private farmland can qualify for assessment and taxation under the Farmland Assessment Act if the land is at least five contiguous acres in area. Land less than five acres may qualify where devoted to agricultural use in conjunction with other eligible acreage under identical legal ownership. To qualify for enrollment, land must produce in excess of 50 percent of the average agricultural production per acre for the given type of land and the given county or area. The acreage requirement may be waived if the owner can show that 80 percent or more of the owner's, buyer's, or lessee's income is derived from agricultural products produced on the land. The production requirement may be waived if the owner shows that the property has been in

(continued)

agricultural use for the previous two years and that failure to meet the production requirement in a particular year was due to no fault or act of the owner, purchaser, or lessee. The production requirement may be waived if the land is involved in a bona fide range improvement program, crop rotation program, or other similarly accepted agricultural practice that does not give reasonable opportunity to satisfy the production level requirement.

Method of UV Assessment:
Productive values are established by the Utah State Tax Commission with the assistance of a Farmland Assessment Advisory Committee and Utah State University. Productive values apply countywide and are based on income and expense factors associated with agriculture activities. These factors are expressed in terms of value per acre for each land classification. Land is classified according to its capability of producing crops or forage. Capability is dependent upon soil type, topography, availability of irrigation water, growing season, and other factors. The county assessor classifies all agricultural land in the county based on SCS Soil Surveys and guidelines provided by the Tax Commission. The general classifications of agricultural land are: irrigated, dry land, grazing land, orchard, and meadow. The state uses a five-year average of commodity prices and a five-year average of crop yields to estimate income from farm use. The capitalization rate used is a five-year moving average of the Federal Land Bank Rate.

Recent Use Values:
In 2012, irrigated farmland was assessed at $893 per acre or less, depending on soil quality and county. Orchard land was assessed in most counties at $600 per acre. Grazing land was assessed at $93 per acre or less. Unproductive land was assessed at $5 per acre in all counties.

Development Penalty:
Yes. When land becomes ineligible for farmland assessment (such as when it is developed or goes into non-use), the owner becomes subject to a rollback tax equal to the difference between the taxes paid while enrolled in the Greenbelt Program and the taxes that would have been paid had the property been assessed at market value. In determining the amount of rollback tax due, a maximum of five years preceding the change in use will be used.

VERMONT

Relevant Statutes:
Vt. Stat. Ann. tit. 32, § 3751 ~ § 3752; Vt. Stat. Ann. tit. 32, § 3755 ~ § 3757

Eligible Uses:
Forestland/Timber Production; Conservation/Open Space; Agricultural/Farmland

Eligibility Requirements:
At least 25 contiguous acres in active agricultural use; or smaller parcels that generate at least $2,000 annually from the sale of farm crops; or actively used agricultural land owned by or leased to a farmer. At least 25 contiguous acres of forestland man-

aged according to state standards and an approved forest management plan. Any land, exclusive of any house site, that is under active conservation management in accord with standards established by the commissioner of forests, parks, and recreation. Eligible farm buildings include all farm buildings and other farm improvements that are actively used by a farmer as part of a farming operation, are owned by a farmer or leased to a farmer under written lease for a term of three years or more, and are situated on land that is enrolled in a use-value appraisal program or on a homesite adjoining enrolled land. Eligible farm buildings are exempt from all property taxes.

Method of UV Assessment:
"Use-value appraisal" means, with respect to land, the price per acre that the land would command if it were required to remain henceforth in agriculture or forest use. With respect to farm buildings, "use-value appraisal" means 0 percent of fair market value.

Recent Use Values:
The 2013 use value for agricultural land is $265 per acre. For forestland a mile or less from a road, the use value is $119 per acre. For less accessible forestland, the assessed use value is $89 per acre.

Development Penalty:
Yes. In the agricultural-use program, development includes: subdivision so that one or more of the resulting parcels is less than 25 acres; construction of buildings, roads, or structures not used for farming purposes; commercial mining, excavation, or landfill activity. In the forest and conservation land program, development includes: subdivision so that one or more of the resulting parcels is less than 25 acres; construction of buildings, roads, or structures not used for forestry purposes; commercial mining, excavation, or landfill activity; or cutting timber contrary to the management plan or contrary to state standards. The land use change tax is calculated as 10 percent or 20 percent of the fair market value of the developed portion prorated on the basis of acreage divided by the common level of appraisal. If land has been enrolled continuously for more than 10 years, the rate is 10 percent. If land has been enrolled 10 years or less, the rate is 20 percent. The obligation to pay this tax runs with the land in perpetuity.

VIRGINIA

Relevant Statutes:
Va. Code Ann. § 58.1-3230 ~§ 58.1-3239

Eligible Uses:
Agricultural/Farmland; Conservation/Open Space; Forestland/Timber Production

Eligibility Requirements:
Chapter 43 of the Code of Virginia, entitled the "Agricultural and Forestal Districts Act," enables any county, city, or town that has adopted a land use plan to adopt an ordinance providing for use-value assessment of qualified land parcels. "Real estate

(*continued*)

devoted to agricultural use" shall mean real estate devoted to the bona fide production for sale of plants and animals useful to man under uniform standards prescribed by the commissioner of Agriculture and Consumer Services. "Real estate devoted to horticultural use" shall mean real estate devoted to the bona fide production for sale of fruits of all kinds, including grapes, nuts, and berries; vegetables; and nursery and floral products. "Real estate devoted to forest use" shall mean land, including the standing timber and trees thereon, devoted to tree growth in such quantity and so spaced and maintained as to constitute a forest area under standards prescribed by the state forester. "Real estate devoted to open-space use" shall mean real estate used as, or preserved for: (1) park or recreational purposes, including public or private golf courses; (2) conservation of land or other natural resources; (3) floodways; (4) wetlands; (5) riparian buffers; (6) historic or scenic purposes; or (7) assisting in the shaping of the character, direction, and timing of community development or for the public interest and consistent with the local land use plan. Land under barns, sheds, silos, cribs, greenhouses, and public recreation facilities shall be included in eligible land. Land used in conjunction with farmhouse or home is not eligible for special assessment: (1) Agricultural or horticultural lands: five acres minimum and must meet standards established by the commissioner of Agriculture & Consumer Services; (2) Forest use: twenty acres minimum and must meet standards established by the state forester; (3) Open-space use: five acres minimum, except that cities, counties, or towns with a population density of greater than 5,000 per square mile may at local option set a minimum of two acres, and must meet standards established by the director of the Department of Conservation and Recreation.

Method of UV Assessment:
The State Land Evaluation Advisory Council shall determine and publish a range of suggested values for each of the several Soil Conservation Service land capability classifications for agricultural, horticultural, forest, and open-space uses in the various areas of the commonwealth. The Advisory Council shall base this determination on productive earning power to be determined by capitalization of warranted cash rents or by the capitalization of incomes of like real estate in the locality or a reasonable area of the locality.

Development Penalty:
Yes. The rollback tax shall be equal to the sum of the deferred tax for each of the five most recent complete tax years including simple interest on such rollback taxes at a rate set by the governing body, no greater than the rate applicable to delinquent taxes in such locality. Localities may adopt a modified version of this rollback penalty. Liability for the rollback taxes shall attach when a change in use occurs or a change in zoning of the real estate to a more intensive use at the request of the owner or his agent occurs.

WASHINGTON

Relevant Statutes:
Wash. Rev. Code § 84.34.020 ~ § 84.34.380; Wash. Admin. Code 458-30-200 ~ 458-30-700

Eligible Uses:
Forestland/Timber Production; Conservation/Open Space; Parks/Recreation; Agricultural/Farmland

Eligibility Requirements:
Farm and agricultural land is defined as any of the following: Any parcel of land that is 20 or more acres, or multiple parcels of land that are contiguous and total 20 or more acres, and are: (1) devoted primarily to the production of livestock or agricultural commodities for commercial purposes; and (2) enrolled in the federal Conservation Reserve Program (CRP). Any parcel of land that is five acres or more, but less than twenty acres, is devoted primarily to agricultural uses, and has produced a gross income equivalent to $200 or more per acre per year for three of the five calendar years preceding the date of application for classification. Any parcel of land five or more acres or multiple parcels of land that are contiguous and total five or more acres that are devoted primarily to the growth and harvest of timber for commercial purposes. Timberland means the land only and does not include a residential house site.

Method of UV Assessment:
If the county legislative authority has established a public benefit rating system (PBRS) for the open-space classification, the criteria contained within the rating system govern the eligibility of the lands described in each application. Open-space land located within a county that has adopted a public benefit rating system will be valued according to the criteria of the rating system. In the absence of a rating system, the valuation will be no less than the lowest per-acre value of classified farm and agricultural land in the county. In determining the current use value of farm and agricultural land, the assessor considers the productive capacity of comparable lands from crops grown most typically in the area averaged over not less than five years. This productive capacity is the "net cash rental" and is capitalized by a rate of interest charged on long-term loans secured by a mortgage on farm or agricultural land plus a component for property taxes. Timberland is valued according to a schedule prepared by the Department of Revenue.

Development Penalty:
Yes. A rollback tax is payable for the last seven years, plus interest at the same rate as charged on delinquent property taxes, plus an additional penalty of 20 percent of the total amount.

WEST VIRGINIA

Relevant Statutes:
W. Va. Code R. § 11-1A-10; W. Va. Code R. §11-1C-10(1); W. Va. Code R. § 11-1C-11 ~ § 11-1C-11b; W. Va. Code R. § 11-13A-3b; W. Va. Code R. §11-3-5

Eligible Uses:
Agricultural/Farmland; Forestland/Timber Production

(*continued*)

Eligibility Requirements:
Forested parcels must be at least 10 acres and must have a forest management plan approved by the Division of Forestry. Use verification must be submitted annually.

Method of UV Assessment:
With respect to farm property, the tax commissioner shall appraise such property so as to ascertain its fair and reasonable value for farming purposes regardless of what the value of the property would be if used for some other purpose, and the value shall be arrived at by giving consideration to the fair and reasonable income that the property might be expected to earn in the locality wherein situated, if rented. The appraised value of managed timberland shall be determined on the basis of the potential of the land to produce future income according to its use and productive potential. Potential future net income is discounted to its present value utilizing a discounted cash flow; this is the appraised value. The ability of a stand of timber to produce wood products for sale or use depends primarily on the quality of the soil and certain topographic and climatic features that can be expressed as a site index. Site index is the principal criterion influencing the appraised value of managed timberland. Farm wood lots shall be included in the valuation of farm property.

Development Penalty:
No penalty applies for farmland that no longer qualifies. For forestland, a penalty applies only if landowner fails to inform assessor of land use change. Penalty for uninformed land use change results in rollback tax for one year.

WISCONSIN

Relevant Statutes:
Wis. Stat. § 70.32(2) ~ § 70.32(4); Wis. Admin. Code Tax § 18.04 ~ § 18.07; Wis. Stat. §77.80~ §77.91; Wis. Stat. § 70.32; Wis. Stat. §74.485; Wis. Stat. §77.01 ~§77.17

Eligible Uses:
Forestland/Timber Production; Wetlands and Other Unproductive Lands; Agricultural/Farmland

Eligibility Requirements:
A property is eligible for the Managed Forest Law (MFL) Program if it has at least 10 contiguous acres covered at least 80 percent by forest dedicated to growing commercial timber. The property cannot be in a registered subdivision. Owners must commit to a 25- or 50-year sustainable forest management plan. A five percent yield tax is due on harvest wood during enrollment in the MFL Program. Land used to grow commercial crops and livestock and Christmas trees or land enrolled in various federal conservation programs is eligible for agricultural use-value assessment.

Method of UV Assessment:
Agricultural land shall be assessed according to the income that could be generated from its rental for agricultural use. Annually, the Department of Revenue determines the average equalized value of an acre of agricultural land in each county in

the previous year and the average fair market value of an acre of agricultural land sold in each county in the previous year based on the sales in each county in the previous year of parcels of agricultural land that are 38 acres or more to buyers who intend to use the land as agricultural land.

Recent Use Values:
MFL land open to public recreation was assessed at $2.14 per acre in 2012. MFL acres closed to public recreation were assessed at $10.68.

Development Penalty:
Yes. When forested land is withdrawn from the MFL Program before expiration of the contract period, the owner owes a penalty calculated in several steps: (1) the net tax rate multiplied by the previous year's assessed land value; and (2) this amount is multiplied by the number of years the land was enrolled in the MFL, then reduced by subtracting any acreage share and yield tax already paid. If agricultural land no longer qualifies for use-value assessment, the owner must pay a conversion charge to the county in which the land is located in an amount that is equal to the number of acres converted multiplied by the amount of the difference between the average fair market value of an acre of agricultural land sold in the county in the year before the year that the person converts the land and the average equalized value of an acre of agricultural land in the county in the year before the year that the person converts the land multiplied by the following:

1. 5 percent, if the converted land is more than 30 acres;
2. 7½ percent, if the converted land is 30 acres or less but at least 10 acres; and
3. 10 percent, if the converted land is less than 10 acres.

WYOMING

Relevant Statutes:
Wyo. Stat. § 39-13-101; Wyo. Stat. § 39-13-102(b); Wyo. Stat. § 39-13-103(x)

Eligible Uses:
Agricultural/Farmland; Forestland/Timber Production

Eligibility Requirements:
"Agricultural land" means land that has been used or employed during the previous two years and presently is being used and employed for the primary purpose of obtaining a monetary profit through agricultural or horticultural use (including timber products or forage) unless legally zoned otherwise by a zoning authority. During the year preceding the assessment year, the owner of nonleased land has derived annual gross revenues of not less than $500 from the marketing of agricultural products, and for leased land, the lessee has derived annual gross revenues of not less than $1,000 from marketing of agricultural products.

Method of UV Assessment:
Wyoming agricultural land is valued according to its capability to produce forage or crops. Agricultural land use is categorized as irrigated cropland, dry cropland, or

(continued)

rangeland. The valuation of agricultural lands involves capitalizing the net operating income the landowner receives from the three categories of agricultural use. Long-term interest rates from the Farm Credit Services of Omaha and effective tax rates are weighted and averaged over a five-year period to obtain the capitalization rate. In 2012, this cap rate was 5.663 percent.

Recent Use Values:
In 2012, the assessed value of irrigated cropland ranged from $32 to $174 per acre. This was 9.5 percent of appraised value because of the Wyoming property classification system.

Development Penalty:
No.

3 \ Theoretical Analyses

It is important to consider the underlying theory of land value determination in order to provide a solid basis for consideration of the taxation of rural and agricultural lands. This chapter begins with land use and land value fundamentals and then addresses the particular application of use-value assessment methods of valuation. Additionally, some of the most important economic impacts of UVA are discussed: impacts on land use conversion, distribution of the tax burden, and capitalization effects.

Theory of Land Value Determinants Within and Beyond a Metropolitan Area

Land use and value fundamentals

What determines land values within and beyond metropolitan regions? Marshall provides fundamental insight on what determines land value in general, highlighting its fixed location characteristic. He states,

> When we have inquired what it is that marks off land from those material things which we regard as products of the land, we shall find that the fundamental attribute of land is its extension. The right to use a piece of land gives command over a certain space—a certain part of the earth's surface. The area of the earth is fixed; the geographic relations in which any particular part of it stands to other parts are fixed. Man has no control over them; they are wholly unaffected by demand; they have no cost of production; there is no supply price at which they can be produced. (1948, 144–145)

Hence, the fundamental determinants of land value are its location and the potential uses for which it may be employed. This is no less true for agricultural and rural land than it is for urbanized land. Given the location of a particular plot of land, its fertility and uses then determine its value.

Ricardian land rent theory

The basic theory of land rent determination goes back to David Ricardo, who wrote in the early part of the nineteenth century. His explanation of land rent determination is summarized in figure 3.1, showing three plots of land of differing fertility used to produce an agricultural product, say, corn.

Plot A is the most fertile of the three plots, reflected in its relatively low cost curves. At the price of corn at least P_1, this plot is drawn into production, and at that price Q_1 units of corn are produced (where price equals marginal cost MC). The producer just breaks even, and the land earns no rent. As the price of corn rises above P_1, corn output increases and land rent is earned on this plot. In the language of the economist, rent refers to the return to a factor of production (land, in this case) that is fixed in supply. Rent is computed as the difference between the commodity price and its average cost of production at the output level where price equals MC times the quantity produced at that price.

If the price of corn rises to at least P_2, then Plot B is drawn into corn production as well. At prices lower than P_2, land of Plot B's fertility is unprofitable, so it will not be used in commodity production. This is the no-rent margin of land use that is known as the *extensive margin*.

Plot B, when used most effectively in the production of corn, will just break even at corn price P_2.

For corn prices above P_2, both plots A and B earn land rents. The extensive margin changes as the commodity price rises, and at a price of corn at least equal to P_3, Plot C is drawn into production. The higher the commodity price, the less fertile the land that will be employed at the extensive margin. If the commodity price were to fall below P_3, then Plot C would be taken out of production and the extensive margin would shift to higher-quality land, namely Plot B. At the high price of P_4, all three plots of land earn rent, illustrated in the shaded rectangles (the distance between the

FIGURE 3.1
Quality of Land and Land Rent Earned

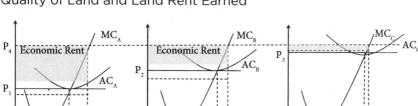

Plot A (Highest-Quality Land)   Plot B (Medium-Quality Land)   Plot C (Poorest-Quality Land)

price and the average cost of production times the quantity of output Q_4),
with the most productive Plot A earning the largest rent and the less productive Plots B and C earning smaller rents.

The dynamics of commodity price increases and their impact on the
extensive margin illustrated in figure 3.1 have been clearly demonstrated
in recent years in grain markets in the United States, for example. With
the national ethanol mandate and other market influences, corn prices
rose to historic levels during the period 2010–2012. The impact of high
corn prices rippled through land markets in corn-producing states. High-
quality corn-producing land earned large economic rents, raising land
prices dramatically. Less productive land was drawn into production as it
began to earn land rents. Land that had formerly been set aside, kept out
of production, and enrolled in the Conservation Reserve Program (CRP)
was withdrawn from that program and brought back into production.

The Ricardian model of land value determination abstracts from location factors and isolates the key elements of value determination taking
location as given. This model makes it clear that land value is determined
by the ability of land to produce marketable products (i.e., fertility, and
thereby cost) at given product prices. The higher the commodity price, the
more valuable the land. The model also makes clear that land use is determined by market forces as well. Only land at the extensive margin, or better,
will be actively used in production. Poorer-quality land will lie fallow. The

extensive margin is based on the market price of a commodity and is subject to change with market conditions.

Another important principle offered by the Ricardian model is that the value of land is determined by the product price. The higher the price of corn, the greater the value of each plot of land will be. Plot A will always be the most valuable because it is the most productive, followed by Plots B and C. A common fallacy in thinking about the relationship between product prices and land prices is that high land prices push up product prices. Yet, the Ricardian model explains that this is not true. It is high product prices that determine high land prices, not the other way around. The more valuable the product being produced, the more valuable the land used in that production.

The effect of UVA in the Ricardian land use context is to shift the extensive margin outward and increase the land area actively used for agricultural production. That would lead to an increased supply of agricultural products that would reduce their price, other things being equal. With lower agricultural commodity prices, land values would be reduced, at least partially offsetting the cost of the UVA program.[1]

Use capacity of land

It is also important to consider the intensity of land use. In economic terms, *land intensity* refers to the amount of capital and labor that is combined with a given amount of land to produce an output (e.g., an agricultural crop, housing services, or commercial/industrial output). The more capital and labor that are applied to the land, the more intensely it is used. Enterprises that use a relatively large of amount of land relative to capital and labor are said to be involved in extensive land uses (not to be confused with the extensive margin previously discussed). Urban land in central commercial districts is used intensively, while farmland is typically used less intensively, and grazing land or forestland is used even less intensely.

The intensive margin of land use is the point reached in cultivation of a crop where the labor or capital being applied to the land just pays its cost.

---

1. To our knowledge, there is not yet any research on this topic.

That is, this margin is the point at which the last unit of labor or capital adds just as much to cost as it does to revenue (MR = MC). The more of the variable input (e.g., capital or labor) that can be used on a given parcel of land before reaching the intensive margin, the more economic capacity the land is said to have.

What affects the intensity of land use? A number of factors are involved. Clearly, land used for industrial or commercial use in an urban area is used more intensely than farmland. The land underneath a high-rise office building in a central city is combined with a substantial amount of capital in the form of a building and equipment in order to produce the business services provided by the firms with offices in the building. That form of land use involves a high degree of capital intensity. Other factors affecting land use intensity include natural characteristics of the land, its location with respect to product markets, and its overall use capacity. Consider the example of high-rise apartment buildings in Hong Kong. Natural topographic features of the island and its coastline limit the amount of land that is buildable, so apartment buildings are very tall and cling to a narrow strip of land near the shore. Additionally, Hong Kong's proximity to mainland China and the rest of Southeast Asia gave it a strategic location advantage with regard to product markets that also contributed to the intensity of land use patterns that developed.

Bid rents and land use

Location factors are now brought back into the picture of land value determination. How land will be used at any given location in an urban area is determined by the rents that may be earned under competing potential land uses. Figure 3.2 illustrates how land use is designated in an urban region where there are three competing land use options. The bid-rent functions illustrate the price that users of land would be willing to bid for land at each location. The commercial bid-rent function is the steepest, as location matters more critically for commercial uses than for residential or agricultural uses. Bid-rent functions are flatter for the residential and agricultural land uses since location is not so important for those uses in comparison to commercial use. At any given distance from the center of the city, the highest

FIGURE 3.2
Bid-Rent Functions and Land Use

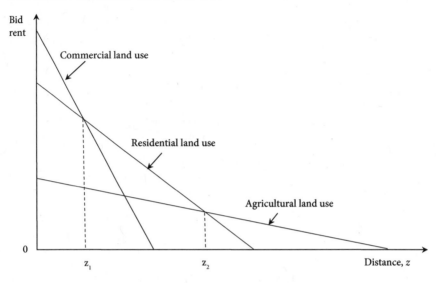

bid-rent curve determines the use for which land is employed. So, for distances within a ring with diameter z_1, land will be used for commercial purposes. Land use changes at distance z_1, and beyond that point land is used for residential purposes. At distance z_2 land use changes to agricultural use, and at any distance beyond that point there is only agricultural land use.

If the bid-rent curve for any of the land uses were to shift, perhaps due to a change in the price of the product produced by that land use (as suggested in Ricardian rent theory), there will be changes in land use. For sake of illustration, suppose that the commercial bid-rent curve shifts upward. That will cause land use to change in the vicinity of z_1, where the land use switch point shifts outward and formerly residential land use will be converted to commercial use. Similarly, if the residential-bid rent curve shifts upward, there will be a change in land use in the vicinity of z_2, where formerly agricultural land will be converted to residential use.[2]

---

2. Zoning ordinances may limit the potential for land use to change around z_1 and z_2. If that is the case, land prices may be substantially affected. In practice, however, zoning regulations may not prevent land use changes in the long run. Zoning laws may follow the land market, with changes in land use dictated by market forces, as illustrated in figure 3.2, eventually adopted in a revised zoning plan.

This model is instructive in thinking about the effect of a reduction in the effective property tax rate for agricultural property. Such a reduction as a result of use-value assessment causes the bid-rent curve for agricultural land use to shift upward. That can theoretically cause land use at the urban periphery to be retained in agricultural use. In a growing urban area, the residential bid-rent curve is shifting upward over time, which by itself would cause land use to change from agriculture to residential use in the vicinity of z_2. Use-value assessment, causing an upward shift in the agricultural bid-rent curve, may have the ability to counteract the urbanization pressure and result in the retention of agricultural land uses and create a stable land use situation in the vicinity of z_2. Whether or not this happens depends upon which bid-rent curve has the larger upward shift.

Property taxes and ways to reduce the property tax burden

There are multiple means by which the effective property tax rate can be reduced for a particular class of properties. The first and most direct way is to implement a classified property tax system in which each class of property can be taxed at its own rate.

The tax liability T for a property is the product of the nominal tax rate t^n and the assessed value AV of the property:

$$T = t^n AV. \tag{1}$$

The assessed value of the property, in turn, is related to its market value MV via the assessment ratio r:

$$AV = rMV. \tag{2}$$

Combining these two relationships gives the tax liability as the product of the nominal tax rate, the assessment ratio, and the market value:

$$T = t^n rMV. \tag{3}$$

We can define the effective tax rate as the product of the nominal tax rate and the assessment ratio:

$$t^e = rt^n, \tag{4}$$

and write the tax liability as the product of the effective tax rate and the market value:

$$T = t^e MV. \tag{5}$$

Hence, we see that the effective tax rate can be altered either by a change in the nominal tax rate or by a change in the assessment ratio.

Methods of reducing the property tax burden must either reduce the nominal tax rate directly or reduce the effective tax rate by reducing the assessment ratio. Some common methods employed by state and local governments include:

- classified tax systems (with lower nominal tax rates for certain classes of property where relief is provided);
- tax exemptions (exempting a portion of assessed value, perhaps for a homestead, thereby reducing the taxable assessed value of the property);
- circuit breakers (providing income-based relief for qualifying properties); and
- use-value assessment provisions (reducing the assessed value for properties where market value exceeds current-use value).

While the focus of this volume is on UVA as a method of reducing property taxes for rural and agricultural property, there are a number of other policy methods for achieving that end, including those listed. UVA is not the only method that can be used.

Use-value assessment (UVA)

All 50 states in the United States provide property tax preferences for agricultural land in some form. Most do so via use-value assessment.[3] Under this assessment method, agricultural land is valued in its current agricultural use, not at its full market value. UVA policy is intended to provide a preferential property tax rate for agricultural and other rural lands that are included in the state's UVA program. Chapter 4 provides a review of

---

3. The 50-state summary is from Bruce and Groover (2007, 1).

the methods used by various states in their application of use-value statutes for rural land. Chapter 5 provides evaluative comments on those methods and makes suggestions for improvements in the methods used. The classic statement on UVA is provided in Gloudemans (1974), who defines UVA as the assessment of property upon the basis of its value in a particular (current) use, rather than upon the basis of its market value.

Assessors generally use an income capitalization approach to assess agricultural use value following the International Association of Assessing Officers (IAAO) standards, which specify that the income approach should be used for agricultural land assessment. IAAO Standard 4.6.5 directs assessors as follows.

> If adequate sales data are available and agricultural property is to be appraised at market value, the sales comparison approach would be preferred. However, nearly every state or province provides for use-value assessment (and usually appraisal), which significantly understates the market value for agricultural property, so the sales comparison approach is usually not applicable. Because of this limitation, *it is imperative to obtain good income data and to use the income approach for agricultural land.* Land rents are often available, sometimes permitting the development and application of overall capitalization rates. This method, of course, also entails the estimation of normal land rents for unrented parcels. When agricultural parcels include improvements, the cost approach or sales comparison models that provide separate building values may be used to determine their value. (IAAO 2008, 11, emphasis added)

In practice, the procedure is to estimate net income generated by agricultural land over some specified period of time and to capitalize that income stream into use value using an appropriate discount rate.

An intriguing alternative possibility for estimating use value arises where there are sufficient data observations on land that is subject to conservation easements. In those cases it may be possible to use market values of land subject to easements to more accurately determine use value. This approach would obviate the need to estimate value using assumed net income data. The limitation, however, is that a sufficient number of market value observations for such land is needed for accurate estimation.

Fundamentals of Land Value

It is important to review the fundamentals of land value to draw careful distinctions regarding its components in order to achieve a precise view of agricultural use value. It is also valuable to discuss the simplified formulas that are used in the computation of use value and the ways that states implement these formulas.

Components of land value

Land value fundamentals have been described by Capozza and Helsley (1989) as consisting of four components: (1) agricultural land value; (2) the value of expected future rent increases; (3) the cost of conversion to developed use; and (4) the value of accessibility. Figure 3.3 illustrates those components in an urban spatial context. The total value of land at any given distance z from the center of a metropolitan region is the sum of these four components, illustrated by the upper contour line. As distance z increases, the value of accessibility declines. The urban land value gradient measures the rate at which land value falls with distance and reflects this fact. Land users who value proximity to the central business district (CBD) are willing to pay a high price for land at close locations. Farther from the CBD, the value of accessibility diminishes.

Urban land within the z^* ring has also been developed with water and sewer lines, street lights, and other features that distinguish it from undeveloped land. The cost of development conversion is the second component of land value. That cost is invariant with respect to distance and is illustrated as constant out to distance z^* and zero thereafter. The third component of urban land value is the value of expected future land rent increases. Landowners expect that urban growth in the future will increase the value of their land within the urbanized zone of the city, that is, within the z^* distance ring around the CBD. The stronger those expectations, the larger

FIGURE 3.3
Fundamentals of Land Value

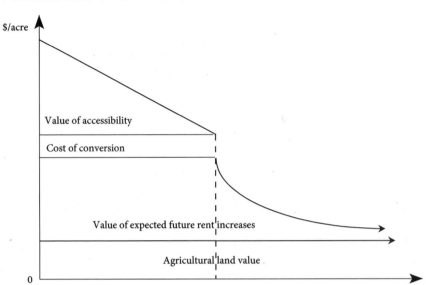

this component of urban land value will be. Of course, those expectations may or may not be fulfilled. Landowners may speculate correctly or incorrectly about future land rent increases. The market for land allows buyers and sellers to act on their expectations and live with the consequences of their decisions. Such behavior facilitates the working of the land market and results in powerful efficiency effects in the allocation of the scarce land resource.

The fourth and final component of urban land value is its agricultural land value. Even if it is not developed or used in a more intensive way, urban land has value in that it is capable of producing agricultural crops or pasture for animals. This component of value is illustrated as a horizontal line in figure 3.3 based on the assumption that the intrinsic fertility of the soil and other features give land at any distance z a foundational value based on its ability to produce agricultural commodities.

At distance z^* where urban development ends, the value of accessibility and the cost–of–conversion components of value drop out and the value of future expected rent increases begins to decline with additional distance. Farther from the CBD, the market value of land approaches its agricultural use value. At sufficiently distant locations from the city center, there is virtually no difference between market value and agricultural use value.

Understanding these components of land value provides insight into how to think about use-value assessment of agricultural land. At very distant locations from the city or in very rural areas, there may be no effective difference between the market value of land and its agricultural use value. Taxing land on the basis of use value rather than market value will have virtually no impact on tax liability. Hence, use-value assessment is unnecessary in this context.

Near the urban fringe, however, there may be a very substantial difference between market value and agricultural use value. At these locations the large difference in value means that use-value assessment will reduce the effective tax rate substantially. Of course, within the urbanized area at distances less than z^*, the land is developed. Even vacant land within this urbanized ring is platted, zoned, or otherwise prepared for developed use. The application of use-value assessment in this area would result in a huge reduction in assessed value due to the large difference between market value and agricultural value. Given that the land has been prepared for development, however, it is inappropriate to apply use-value assessment to such property.

So what, exactly, is agricultural use value?

If we isolate the particular components of land value related to undeveloped agricultural land, we have components (1) and (2) listed. That is, agricultural use value is the combination of the pure agricultural value of land and the expected future rent increases that may be relevant, depending on location. The second component is relevant near the urban border and decays with distance from the city.

In this case, the agricultural land price is simply the sum of the capitalized values of the agricultural rent stream and the expected value of future rent changes. This view of agricultural land value recognizes that the land is valuable both for its ability to generate a stream of net rental income and also for the possibility that future growth will increase the rent-earning ability of the land. If we take a more narrow view of the agricultural land value, we ignore the expected future rent increases due to growth and designate the agricultural land value as only the first component—the capitalized net agricultural rent. In that case, land value can be written as the familiar perpetuity formula where the agricultural land price is the annual net income $\tilde{A}$ divided by the discount rate r.

$$P^a(t) = \frac{\tilde{A}}{r}. \tag{6}$$

In the presence of a property tax system, the familiar perpetuity formula must also include the property tax rate (τ) to account for the capitalization of the tax into the land price.

$$P^a(t) = \frac{\tilde{A}}{(r+\tau)}. \tag{7}$$

Case studies illustrating the difference between market value and use value

In order to illustrate the impact of use-value assessment, consider the case studies provided in Anderson and Griffing (2000a, 2000b). They estimated the difference between market value and use value for agricultural land surrounding the two largest urban areas in Nebraska as illustrated in figure 3.3, confirming the pattern illustrated. They found that the difference between market value and use value declines with distance from the center of Lincoln for a sample of land parcels in Lancaster County and from the center of Omaha for a sample of parcels in the southwesterly direction from Omaha in Sarpy County. Table 3.1 reports their estimated value difference at various distances from Lincoln and Omaha.

Moving out from the center of Lincoln, the difference between market value and use value declines from $988 per acre at three miles (the minimum distance in the sample) to $89 per acre at 24 miles. The mean ratio of use value to market value around Lincoln was about 0.64, indicating that use-value assessment reduced taxable value by about 36 percent. The

TABLE 3.1

Market and Use Values for Land Parcels Around Lincoln and Omaha, Nebraska

	Lincoln, Lancaster County	Omaha, Sarpy County
Distance (Miles) : Difference between market value and use value ($/acre)	3 : $988	6 : $6,386
	10 : $444	10 : $4,343
	20 : $141	20 : $1,657
	24 : $89	25 : $1,024
Mean ratio of use value to market value	0.639	0.2477
Mean distance (miles)	13.04	16.47
Mean parcel size (acres)	86.37	72.05
Gradient of difference between market value and use value	0.115	0.093

SOURCE: Anderson and Griffing (2000a, 2000b).

estimated gradient of 0.115 indicates that the spatial rate of decay in the difference between market value and use value with respect to distance is 11.5 percent. That means for each additional mile farther from the city center, the difference in values is reduced by 11.5 percent.

For Omaha, the difference in value declines from $5,386 per acre at six miles (the minimum distance in the sample) to $1,024 at twenty-four miles. The mean ratio of use value to market value around Omaha was about 0.25, indicating that use-value assessment reduced taxable value by about 75 percent. The estimated gradient of 0.093 indicates that the spatial rate of decay in the difference between market value and use value with respect to distance is 9.3 percent. That means for each additional mile farther from the city center, the difference in values is reduced by 9.3 percent.

Highest and best value

Property tax assessment practice based on market value principles begins with the assumption of what assessors call *highest and best use* of the property. That is, the assessor is supposed to ignore the current use of the property and make an assumption about the use that would generate the largest possible net revenue. Barlowe's (1978) definition of highest and best use in his classic text on land economics is: "Land resources are at their highest and best use when they are used in such a manner as to provide the optimum return to their operators or to society" (16).

In practice, assessors can readily see a parcel's current use, but they must speculate whether it is actually the highest and best use of the parcel. In some cases it is easy to see that it is not. Consider, for example, a flat, paved parking lot in the center of a high-rise downtown area. It is quite likely that the highest and best use of the parking-lot land is a developed commercial use instead. In other cases it may be quite difficult to ascertain whether highest and best use differs from current use. In those cases, it may well be that assessors are implicitly biased in favor of accepting current use as highest and best use. Moreover, that bias may be appropriate given the uncertainty facing the assessor.

Ultimately, current market values capture the information required and do not involve subjective judgments. Hence, this work focuses on market values and the information content embedded in those prices.

Calculating use value

The factors needed to estimate agricultural use value are given in equation (7), which indicates that we need an estimate of the net income $\tilde{A}(t)$ and an appropriately selected capitalization rate plus property tax rate: $(r + \tau)$. The choice of both numerator and denominator involves potential problems and complications. As Bunnell (1996) puts it, at this point an idea that is simple in principle becomes complicated in practice.

Several basic definitional issues must be addressed. First, the very definition of agricultural or rural land use must be articulated. Our 50-state review of UVA statutes reveals great variation in the definitions used. If the intent of the UVA legislation is to assist farmers and ranchers, then the definition of eligible land would be restricted to land actually in commercial agricultural production, for crops or cattle. Swampland, forestland, or idle farmland would not be included under the eligibility criteria. Some states specifically apply UVA to forestland and/or open space, however.

In order to objectively identify agricultural land, it might seem reasonable to require that the land be zoned agricultural. This is not always the case, however, as in many rural areas there is no zoning. Even in rural areas with zoning, however, some UVA statutes do not require that land be zoned agricultural in order to receive UVA tax treatment. Bunnell (1996) indicates that some states, such as Wisconsin, do not have any specific zoning requirement for UVA eligibility. In such a case, agricultural land could qualify for UVA despite being zoned for commercial development and despite plans for development having been submitted and approved by the local planning commission.

Eligibility requirements have an impact on how UVA should be computed. In the case cited here, where no zoning requirement is included in the statute, a broader estimate of value may be appropriate. In terms of the components of land value listed here, the second component (the value of expected future rent increases) should be included in this situation.

Another example of how eligibility requirements may affect the computation of UVA is when the statute does not require a minimum parcel size. In that case, small parcels may qualify for UVA, whereas those parcels may actually be residential acreages in rural areas or urban parcels with small gardens in the city.

Some state UVA statutes do not include improvements in the value definition. In those cases, structures such as farmhouses, silos, and barns are assessed separately. Separate assessment of the structures may not be a simple matter, however. Farmhouses, outbuildings, and other structures may be difficult to assess using a market comparison approach if few comparables (e.g., farmhouses sold separately from farmland) are available. Furthermore, it may be that the barns, silos, and other farm structures are economically obsolete and effectively worthless in terms of their current ability to produce agricultural income. Still, they may retain aesthetic value for some buyers. It is also possible that the structures are so depreciated that they actually have negative value. That is, the property would have higher value if they were removed. Fundamentally, the problem of disentangling the value of the marginal product of structures is a classic problem in land value assessment.

As captured in equation (7), there are two fundamental entities to be estimated in determining use value: first, the net revenue stream; second, an appropriate capitalization rate.

Estimating net income

The first number required to compute agricultural use value is an estimate of the net income stream generated by agricultural land. Most states require the use of some form of equation (7) to estimate use value, so the first consideration is how to estimate the numerator of that equation. The simplest version of equation (7) is a plain perpetuity, assuming a constant amount of net income is generated each year, forever. In that case we need an estimate of the representative annual net income generated by the land. Net income is gross income generated via agricultural production minus the cost of inputs used in that production. This measure of net income should be a broad measure, including all of the sources of net income that are attributable to the agricultural or rural use of the land and other real property. A narrow measure of net income, such as that which might be reported on IRS Form 1040's Schedule F, has the effect of understating the use value of the property.

States often specify assessment methods that use estimates of agricultural productivity for various commonly planted crops as the starting point to estimate gross revenue. For example, in Iowa land parcels are rated by the corn suitability index, reflecting the major crop produced in the state. With an assumed productivity per acre of land (perhaps adjusted for soil quality, topography, and other conditions) and commodity price data, an estimate of total revenue can be computed. Assumed costs of production can then be netted out to obtain an estimate of net income per acre. Rather than use a single year's data as representative, however, many states require that a moving average of several years of income and cost data be used to estimate a representative net income in equation (7). Several detailed examples of the way that states estimate net income are included in chapter 4.

Because rental data are often readily available for agricultural land, assessors sometimes begin their estimation of net income by using the annual rent paid for use of the land. While that number may be more readily available than other income data, it may not be appropriately representative. The assessor must assess all agricultural land parcels, whether rented to a tenant farmer or farmed by the owner. This raises the difficulty that rented parcels may systematically differ in some way from nonrented parcels used in agricultural production. It may be that landowners are reluctant to rent out prime agricultural land to tenant operators whose land-stewardship practices may differ from the owner's, which would result in only inferior-quality land being rented. Or it may be that rented land is more likely not to be irrigated and therefore will be less productive. Despite this potential difficulty, assessors often use rental incomes as their starting point for all parcels. Gross rents are then adjusted by deducting estimates of the cost of inputs.

Another complication in using rental income is that the very presence of a differential method of taxation has an economic impact on the land use. Keene et al. explain the issue this way:

> In many areas . . . rental values are distorted by the very existence of differential assessment. Investors and developers are willing to rent out land to a nearby farmer for little more than the real property taxes attributable to the land, so as to qualify it as agricultural land in order to obtain the benefits of differential assessment. Observed rents in such situations may bear little relationship to the economic surplus attributable to the land in agricultural use. (1976, 35)

The problem is that land rents may systematically differ in areas where use-value assessment is permitted. This difficulty in estimation is the econometric issue of endogeneity, which requires statistical methods of correction. Future research is needed to develop proper methods to correct for this conceptual difficulty.

Choosing a discount rate

Application of equation (7) to estimate use value requires the choice of an appropriate discount rate to use in the denominator. Ultimately, the discount rate should reflect the opportunity cost of capital. While that sounds like an easy task, it is not. Economists decompose the discount rate into five components: a riskless rate (r*), an inflation premium (IP), a default risk premium (DRP), a liquidity premium (LP), and a maturity risk premium (MRP).

$$r = r^* + IP + DRP + LP + MRP \tag{8}$$

Anderson (2012) discusses which of these factors should be included in the discount rate and how to estimate use value. He indicates that if the income stream is nominal (measured in current dollars) and covers several years, then the appropriate discount rate should include both the risk-free rate and the expected rate of inflation over the same period (an inflation premium). Of course, the interest rate chosen should also match the term structure with the time period used for the income measure in the numerator of equation (7). A DRP term is generally not needed because the interest rate chosen as the starting point in (8) already incorporates default risk. An LP term and/or an MRP term may be appropriate to include in the discount rate as well, depending on the base rate chosen.

Proper choice of the discount rate is critical to accurate use-value assessment. If an artificially high discount rate is chosen, the use-value estimate will be biased downward. A review of commonly used discount rate choice methods reported in Anderson (2012) indicates that states often use high discount rates. Chapter 4 presents six case studies that highlight the discount rate choice, among other critical estimation issues.

Theory of Economic Impacts of Use-Value Assessment

Impacts on land use conversion

One of the motivating factors for implementing UVA is to delay conversion to developed uses, thereby temporarily preserving open space and prime agricultural land. Whether and to what extent such delay may occur has been the subject of a number of studies. Preferential tax treatment of land may have an impact on both the timing of eventual development and the capital intensity of that development. Skouras (1978) and Anderson (1986) have explored the theoretical possibilities. A well-known result in public finance is that, if the property tax is unrelated to current land use, the tax has no effect on the timing of development or its capital intensity, and is therefore neutral (Tideman 1982). If, however, the property tax is related to current land use as a result of assessment practices biased in favor of current use, it may well be non-neutral in its effects. Anderson (1993b) provides analysis of the potential impacts of UVA on land use, land value, timing, and capital intensity of development. He shows that under certain circumstances there can be impacts on both the timing of development, with UVA delaying development, and on the capital intensity of land development. Of course, there are also direct impacts on the tax burden and on land values.

Impacts on the tax burden

Use-value assessment reduces tax liability for owners of eligible land parcels and thereby creates a tax expenditure (an expenditure made by the local government via the tax system rather than via direct outlay). In effect, state and local governments are spending money on preserving open space or prime agricultural land, general assistance to farmland owners, or whatever the stated objective of the UVA program may be. The size of that tax expenditure can be substantial in areas where the difference between market value and use value is large. Large tax expenditures occur near the periphery of urban areas.

Anderson and Griffing (2000b) found that the tax expenditure associated with use-value assessment is quite substantial in the metro areas of Lincoln and Omaha, Nebraska. Their estimates indicate that the tax expenditure for land parcels given UVA tax treatment is approximately 36 percent of total revenue that would have otherwise been collected on those parcels in Lancaster County, Nebraska, and 75 percent that in Sarpy County, Nebraska.

Whether the reduced tax burden is sufficient to prevent farmland from being developed is questionable, however. The value of the tax savings due to UVA may well be swamped by the potential gain from selling rural land on the metropolitan fringe to a developer. For a given level of public expenditure by the local government units relying on the property tax (school district, city, county, etc.), the preferential tax treatment for UVA land causes property tax rates to be higher for all other property owners in the jurisdiction. Hence, UVA causes a tax shift from agricultural land-owners to residential, commercial, and industrial landowners. Therein lies a substantial social cost of UVA programs.

Impacts on land values (capitalization)

Because UVA reduces the tax liability on a parcel of land, while the services provided by the local government are presumed to remain constant, the lower tax liability is capitalized into a higher land value. In terms of equation (7), a lower effective tax rate in the denominator increases the value of the land. Land subject to preferential tax treatment such as UVA will have a higher value, other things being equal.

At the point when UVA legislation is passed and this preferential tax method goes into effect, the value of land jumps up by the capitalized value of the future stream of reduced taxes. That confers a wealth increase to the landowner at the time of UVA adoption. Subsequent sales of the land occur with knowledge of the UVA tax regime and anticipation (appropriate or not) of its continuation. Hence, subsequent buyers are unaffected. UVA has no further impact on land values after the first sale subsequent to UVA adoption. Any change in a UVA program to either expand or scale back the program will confer windfall gains or losses to current landowners, making such changes politically difficult. Proposals to scale back a UVA program will be met with resistance by current landowners who would suffer capital losses. On the other hand, policy makers who are contemplating the adoption or expansion of a UVA program will find support from current landowners who would benefit from a windfall gain in land value.

Anderson (1993a) modeled the capitalization effects of preferential tax treatment of agricultural land (via a circuit breaker) and identified the factors determining the size of the initial effect. He found that for a given farm income stream and a given potential development income stream, the capitalization effect is larger: (1) the greater the effective property tax rate; (2) the lower the discount rate; and (3) the more generous the preferential tax mechanism (circuit breaker income threshold).

Summary and Conclusions

This chapter provides the theoretical basis for understanding land value determination and offers a framework for considering UVA application and impacts. Ricardian land rent theory explains how land rents and land values are generated by the profitability of producing commodities using the land. High agricultural commodity prices, for example, result in higher land rents being earned on cultivated land parcels and therefore higher land values. In addition, high commodity prices draw marginal lands into production. In this way, the theory describes both the extensive and intensive margins of land use, explaining both what type of land is used and how intensively any given parcel is used.

The chapter examines urbanized area situations and shows how spatial land value patterns apply, with market values high near the CBD and declining with distance out past the urbanized fringe and approaching pure agricultural land value beyond the developed city area. This model provides insight into the potential impacts of UVA when applied to undeveloped land parcels in an urban area where the market value of the land is well above its agricultural use value.

A simple computational model of use value has also been presented illustrating the fundamental estimations required in determining use value for tax purposes. UVA requires estimates of the net income flow generated by the land parcel and an estimate of the opportunity cost of capital in order to compute the capitalized value of the income stream. The mechanics of use-value estimation presented here form the basis for evaluating the practices employed by assessors in chapter 4.

The result of UVA in an urban region where market values exceed use values is a substantial reduction in the property tax on the land, which may delay its conversion to developed use as intended by the UVA program. But the application of UVA also causes a tax shift to other landowners and thereby creates a social cost that must be considered as an unintended consequence.

APPENDIX 3.1

The Mathematics of Land Values

Capozza and Helsley (1989) (hereafter CH) express the price of developed land at time t and location z in an urban area, P^d (t, z), as the sum of the four components listed here:

$$P^d(t,z)=\frac{A}{r}+C+\left(\frac{1}{r}\right)\left(\frac{T}{\bar{L}}\right)[\bar{z}(t)-z]+\left(\frac{1}{r}\right)\int_t^\infty R_u(u,z)e^{-r(u-t)}du. \tag{1}$$

The first term in this expression, $\frac{A}{r}$, is the capitalized value of the annual agricultural rent stream, assumed to be a perpetuity. This is the pure agricultural value of the property based solely on the capitalized net income generated. The second term, C, is the cost of development conversion capturing the investment in capital improvements to the land. The Capozza and Helsley model implicitly assumes that C applies only to land prepared for developed use. In reality, agricultural land is also improved in various ways with capital investments for drainage (tiling), outbuildings, and other improvements. As a consequence, the A term should be considered to be net of capital expenses as well other expenses. These first two terms are invariant to location z; hence they are shown as horizontal lines in figure 3.1. The third term, $\left(\frac{1}{r}\right)\left(\frac{T}{\bar{L}}\right)[\bar{z}(t)-z]$, is the value of accessibility to the city center. This term depends on transportation cost T and the mean lot size $\bar{L}$. As a result, this term declines with distance z to the CBD, which is expressed as $[\bar{z}(t)-z]$. The final term in the CH model is $\left(\frac{1}{r}\right)\int_t^\infty R_u(u,z)e^{-r(u-t)}du$, which captures the value of expected future rent increases that are caused by population growth in the urban area, which is an expected growth premium. Land rents may rise in the future as a result of general growth in the urban area, thus creating an increase in land value. This term can be substantial in size within the urbanized area, but it declines in size beyond the developed area of the city. Hence, figure 3.3 illustrates this term decaying beyond the urbanized ring (i.e., beyond the city boundary z^*).

Analysis of land value determination can begin with the case where the current land use determined by the market is the highest and best use, and there is no possibility for development or redevelopment in the future. This is an extreme case, but it enables a focus on the basic mechanics of property value determination.

Assuming that the net revenue stream generated by the current market use is $A(t)$ and that the discount rate is r, the estimated value of the property at time $V(t)$ can be written as

$$V(t)=\int_0^\infty A(u)e^{-r(u-t)}du. \tag{2}$$

In this expression e is the exponential function used to discount the revenue stream in continuous time.

If we incorporate a property tax applied at the rate τ in the model,

$$V(t) = \int_0^\infty A(u)e^{-(r+\tau)(u-t)}du. \tag{3}$$

This expression indicates that with a property tax included in the model, the discount rate appropriate for use in discounting the revenue stream has two elements: an interest rate and the property tax rate.

Now, by restricting the view of net revenue generated by the property to the value in current agricultural use, we can denote the restricted net revenue stream as $\tilde{A}(t)$ and write the agricultural use value as

$$\tilde{V} = \int_0^\infty \tilde{A}(u)e^{-ru}du. \tag{4}$$

This expression assumes that the agricultural land generates revenue of $\tilde{A}(t)$ in perpetuity, that is, forever. By including a property tax applied to the land, the approximation to (3) can be written as the simple perpetuity formula

$$\tilde{V} = \frac{\tilde{A}}{r+\tau}, \tag{5}$$

where the capitalization rate is the sum of the discount rate and the tax rate: $(r+\tau)$. This equation suggests that states using an income capitalization approach should estimate net agricultural income for the numerator and use a combined interest rate plus property tax rate for the capitalization rate in the denominator.

4 \ Empirical Studies
of Implementation and Impacts

This chapter considers the practices that states actually use to calculate use value of rural and agricultural property. Six case studies—Indiana, Iowa, Kansas, Ohio, Virginia, and Wisconsin—illustrate several prototype methods used in implementing UVA programs. The implementation and impacts of these programs involve enrollment criteria, preservation of small family farms and rural landscapes, shifting of the property tax burden and equity, and property tax administration.

Empirical Practices Used by States

The data needed to actually estimate agricultural use value were identified in equation (5) of chapter 3. What is required is both an estimate of the annual net income $\tilde{A}(t)$ from agricultural use of a land parcel and an appropriate capitalization rate $(r+\tau)$, including the property tax rate.

Most states confront the averaging issue in one way or another. The simple perpetuity formula, whereby land value is computed as the quotient of annual net income divided by the capitalization rate (including property tax rate), given by $V(t) = \dfrac{\tilde{A}(t)}{(r+\tau)}$, assumes that net income in year t is repeated every year forever into the future. In reality, with respect to agricultural land, the income stream fluctuates from year to year. Furthermore, the discount rate and property tax rate also fluctuate over time. Consequently, states generally provide guidance to assessors regarding methods to use in smoothing both the income data and the discount and property tax rates via some type of averaging method. Table 4.1 reports the capitalization rates employed by most of the states with UVA programs.

TABLE 4.1

Capitalization Rates Used by States in Computing
Agricultural Use Value

State	Capitalization Rate Computation
Alabama	Ten-year average New Orleans District Federal Land Bank (FLB) loan rate
Alaska	NA
Arizona	Five-year average FLB rate + 1.5%
Arkansas	Rate determined by Assessment Coordination Department using long-term federal security rates, risk rates, management rates, and other appropriate financial rates, constrained to be within the interval [8%, 12%]
California	Four-year mean of the yield rate for long-term U.S. government bonds adjusted for other factors, including components for risk, property taxes, and amortization
Colorado	Statutory 13% rate
Florida	Five-year average capitalization rate using band-of-investment approach plus property tax rate
Hawaii	NA
Idaho	Five-year average of the Spokane office of the Farm Credit System plus a component for the local tax rate
Illinois	Five-year average FLB rate
Indiana	Computed from Chicago FRB real estate loan and operating loan interest rates
Iowa	7%
Kansas	Five-year average FLB rate + add-on of at least 0.75% and not more than 2.75% (determined by director of property valuation) + county average property tax rate. Statute specifies that the first two components of the above computation must be at least 11%, but not more than 12%
Kentucky	Ten-year average of mortgage interest rates obtained from Farm Credit Services and IRS rules + return on investor's equity developed from farm income divided by actual farm sales + statewide effective property tax rate
Louisiana	Max [12%, calculated rate], where calculated rate = risk-free rate + 2.33% risk component + 0.16% nonliquidity component
Maine	NA

State	Capitalization Rate Computation
Maryland	Computation in 1999: 9% − 2% for inflation + 5% for capital market imperfection + 1% effective property tax rate = 13%
Massachusetts	Five-year average FLB rate
Michigan	NA
Minnesota	NA
Mississippi	Calculated rate, but not less than 10%
Montana	6.4% unless different rate is recommended by Advisory Committee
Nebraska	Rate shall include, but not be limited to, an appropriate discount rate for the land use of the parcel of land, an adjustment for change in land value, and the effective tax rate for the parcel of land
Nevada	NA
New Hampshire	NA
New Jersey	10%
New Mexico	Cap rate is established for five-year period of use, based on FLB and PCA rates
New York	10% (8% presumed discount rate plus 2% presumed property tax rate)
North Carolina	Calculated rate, constrained to be within the interval [6%, 7%]
North Dakota	12-year trimmed average of St. Paul FLB rate, computed by omitting highest and lowest rates, averaging remaining 10 years' rates
Ohio	60% of five-year average Farm Credit Services fifteen-year interest rate + 40% of five-year average interest rate on equity + expected future five-year average depreciation or appreciation + five-year average state property tax rate
Oklahoma	65% of five-year average FLB rate + 17.5% of five-year average second mortgage rate + 17.5% of five-year average CD rate + county effective tax rate
Oregon	Five-year average Oregon Federal Farm Credit Bank rate + effective property tax rate
Pennsylvania	NA
South Carolina	FLB rate + effective local tax rate + risk adjustment of 15% + 0.3% for nonliquidity

(continued)

State	Capitalization Rate Computation
South Dakota	6.6%
Tennessee	Rate = total farm real estate interest expense divided by total farm real estate debt as published by Tennessee agricultural statistics service, +/− 0.1% to reflect differences in land classes within a jurisdiction
Texas	Five-year average rate, max [10%, FLB rate + 2.5%]
Utah	Five-year average FLB rate
Vermont	NA
Virginia	10-year average of Agricultural Credit Association interest rate + 10-year average of effective true property tax rate + risk adjustment (optional)
Washington	Five-year average of Farm Credit Administration and other large financial institutions rate + property tax rate
West Virginia	Riskless rate + risk adjustment + nonliquidity adjustment + management rate + statewide effective property tax rate
Wisconsin	Max [11%, five-year average of one-year ARM agricultural loan rates + municipal tax rate]
Wyoming	Five-year average Omaha FLB rate

Most states use moving averages of both net income and the capitalization rate, although the methods specified by state statutes and regulations vary greatly. At the outset, it is also important to note that, when one calculates the average of the sum of quotients, it is not equal to the quotient of sums. That is, if we average the valuation ratio over n years, we will get a different answer than if we take the ratio of the n-year average of net income and divide by the n-year average discount rate (including property tax rate).

In order to see how averaging specifications and methods yield different results, consider the annual rates of change for nonirrigated farmland in the 10th District of the Federal Reserve System. Figure 4.1 illustrates the rates of change over the period 1986–2012. Three averages for the rate of change in nonirrigated land value are illustrated: (1) the rate of change in land value in year t is the average of the previous six years' annual rates

FIGURE 4.1

Alternate State Averaging Methods Applied to Federal Reserve 10th District Nonirrigated Land Value Rates of Change, Annual Percent Changes, 1986–2012

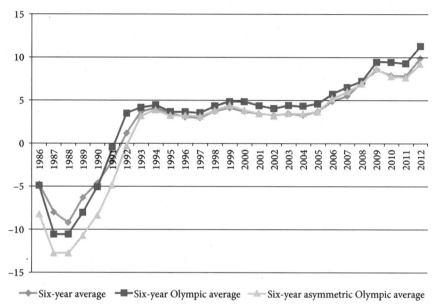

—◆— Six-year average   —■— Six-year Olympic average   —▲— Six-year asymmetric Olympic average

SOURCE: Author's computations are based on nonirrigated agricultural land value data from the Federal Reserve Bank of Kansas City (2013).

NOTE: The area of the 10th Federal Reserve District includes Colorado, Kansas, Nebraska, Oklahoma, Wyoming, the northern half of New Mexico, and the western third of Missouri.

of change; (2) the rate of change in land value in year *t* is an Olympic average of the past six years' rates of change, with both the high and low values omitted; and (3) the rate of change in land value in year *t* is an asymmetric Olympic average, with only the high value omitted. The data used in this computation begin in 1980 and capture the effects of the farm crisis when land values were falling dramatically. However, because of the six-year averaging window, figure 4.1 begins in 1986.

The patterns illustrated reveal the effects of the farm crisis with negative rates of change in land values until the 1991–1992 period. When we compared the six-year moving average, the Olympic average, and the asymmetric Olympic average, it is clear that the asymmetric Olympic average consistently provides the lowest estimates. This result is no surprise, because that average systematically omits the largest rate of change in any six-year window of time. Interestingly, the Olympic average is below the full six-year average during periods of falling land values, but above that average during periods of rising land values.

Six Case Studies

Indiana

Indiana provides preferential tax treatment for agricultural property, classified forest/timber, and wild lands. Preferential tax treatment is delivered through current-use valuation of these property categories. The Department of Local Government Finance is directed by statute to give written notice to each county assessor of the USDA's soil survey data and the appropriate productivity factor for each type or classification of soil shown in the survey. Those data are then used to determine the true tax value of agricultural land.

Indiana's agricultural land base-rate calculation was established in 2002 as a response to a 1998 state Supreme Court case (*State Board of Tax Commissioners v. Town of St. John*). That case found the previous system of property taxation based on so-called "true tax value" to be unconstitutional because it violated the uniformity requirement of the state constitution. Following that decision, the Department of Local Government Finance and the General Assembly developed new assessment rules based on market value for nonagricultural properties and use value for agricultural properties. The *Town of St. John* case affirmed that use-value assessment for agricultural land is constitutional. Prior to that case, the agricultural base rate was determined via negotiation between the State Tax Board and an agricultural advisory council. Prior to 2003 the base rate was $495/acre. With the change in market valuation methodology in 2003 using an income capitalization method and a four-year average, the base rate more than doubled to $1,050. Since 2007 the computation has been based on a six-year moving average of net income and capitalization rates.

Table 4.2 lists the Indiana base value rates and the averaging method used from 2003 to 2013. The values are computed by dividing an average

TABLE 4.2
Indiana Base Land Value Rates, 2003–2013

Year	Moving Average	Years of Data Used in Calculation	Base Rate ($/acre)
Prior to 2003			495
2003–2005	4-year average	1999–2002	1,050
2006	4-year average	2000–2003	880
2007	6-year average	1999–2004	880
2008	6-year average	2000–2005	1,140
2009	6-year average	2001–2006	1,200
2010	6-year average	2002–2007	1,250
2011	6-year average, omitting highest value	2003–2008	1,290
2012	6-year average, omitting highest value	2004–2009	1,500
2013	6-year average, omitting highest value	2005–2010	1,630

SOURCES: Purdue University (2010) and Indiana Department of Local Government Finance (2013).

NOTE: These base values determine taxes in the year listed, which are actually paid in the following year.

of net income by an average capitalization rate. Starting in 2011, the six-year average method was modified to eliminate the highest value during the six-year period, an asymmetric Olympic mean. By 2013, the base valuation per acre had risen to $1,630.

The Indiana Real Property Assessment Guidelines specify that an average net income is to be capitalized by an average capitalization rate. The Department of Local Government Finance *Certification of Agricultural Land Base Rate Value for Assessment Year 2012* specifies, "The capitalization rate applied to both types of net income (cash rent and owner-occupied production) was based on the annual average interest rate on agricultural real estate and operating loans in Indiana for this same period" (2). For 2012, the computed capitalization rate was 6.17 percent. The net income data are provided by the Purdue Agricultural Economics Report, which reports both land values and rents. Data on crop yields, crop prices, and costs are obtained from this source and used to compute an average net income. The Department of Local Government Finance provides an estimate of property tax payments per acre, and that amount is subtracted from the net income figures used in the numerator of the valuation formula. The computed base rate for tax year 2013 (payable in 2014) is $1,760 per acre.

Once the base rate B is computed, it is then adjusted to suit particular parcels through the use of two adjustment factors. First, a soil productivity factor S, provided by the Purdue University Department of Agricultural Economics, is applied, where $0.50 \leq S \leq 1.28$. This factor is intended to capture the soil productivity and its impact on the income-earning capacity of the agricultural land parcel being assessed. The *adjusted rate* is then the product of the base rate and the soil productivity index S. Second, another adjustment is made using an *influence factor I*, where $0 \leq I \leq 1$, which captures factors reducing the productivity of the land. So, the use value of an acre is finally the product of the base rate B, the soil productivity index S, and the influence factor I: $\tilde{V} = BSI$. For special types of land use, such as classified forestland, wildlife habitats, and windbreaks, Indiana permits lower assessments, as low as one dollar per acre.

In addition to the preferential assessment method described, which reduces the effective property tax rate for agricultural land, Indiana also has property tax caps that were enacted in 2008 and implemented in 2009. Those caps limit the tax bill on farmland to 2.5 percent of gross assessed value. Starting in 2010, those caps were tightened to 2.0 percent of gross assessed value.

Iowa

Iowa provides preferential tax treatment for agricultural land, conservation lands or open space, forest or timberlands, and other land uses. Those preferences are provided via a combination of current-use valuation, different assessment ratios, and values determined by the state. Agricultural land is assessed based on its use value using an income capitalization approach. The Iowa methodology includes particular ways to estimate use value based on soil productivity, with particular reference to corn productivity. Assessors are directed to first undertake studies of income capitalization, and then to apply the results of those studies to individual tracts of land to determine actual value. Such studies must place their focus on the determination of net income, because Iowa Code Section 441.21, paragraph 1.*e*, specifies a fixed 7 percent capitalization rate to be used for agricultural property.

The *Iowa Real Property Appraisal Manual* (Iowa Department of Revenue 2008) points out, "The analysis of individual tracts of land not only permits the income data to be applied to each tract, but also can determine the existence of certain factors which can affect the value of a particular tract of land" (2-24). The manual further prescribes that four groups of factors be considered in valuation: (1) soil productivity; (2) presence of buildings; (3) land location; and (4) other factors. Soil maps that record soil and erosion characteristics of land are used to determine the productive capability of particular parcels to be assessed. Average temperatures and precipitation by region of the state are also considered in judging productive capability of land.

A Corn Suitability Rating (CSR) is assigned to each soil map unit. CSR ratings range from 5 to 100, where a CSR of 100 indicates soils with high-yield potential located in the most favorable weather conditions in the state that can be row cropped continuously with little erosion. The CSR is then the foundational basis for assessment, with adjustments made to account for special considerations. Examples of such special considerations include isolated small areas, areas with poor drainage, areas subject to flooding, areas covered by scattered timber or brush, and areas that are heavily timbered.

A complicating factor that arises in Iowa is the assessment of building value on agricultural land. While the *Iowa Real Property Appraisal Manual* specifies that buildings be valued at market value, it then specifies that an agricultural factor must be determined and applied to the market value. The manual specifies that "the agricultural factor for each jurisdiction is calculated as the product of the ratio of the productivity and net earning capacity value per acre ... over the market value of agricultural land within the assessing jurisdiction" (7-1). Previously, Iowa used a three-year moving average to smooth assessments. Starting in 2013, however, Iowa is implementing a five-year average of values to determine the agricultural factor.

Two related assessment issues arise with the Iowa use-value assessment procedures. The first involves the assessment of agricultural buildings. The Iowa procedure requires a reduction in the building value below its market value. The manual provides an example of assessing an agricultural building with market value of $500,000 and an agricultural factor of 30 percent, resulting in a productivity value for the building of $150,000 (30 percent of $500,000). Hence, the Iowa policy is not only to tax the land in its use value rather than market value, but also to tax agricultural buildings at less than their full market value. The value of buildings is reduced by the agricultural factor derived from a land-productivity estimation procedure, which in theory is unrelated to the value of structures. Second, the Iowa procedure prevents the assessor from recognizing distinct land uses on an agricultural parcel. The manual specifies, "An assessor shall not value a part of the land as agricultural real estate and a part of the land as if it is residential real estate" (71-1). In other words, this extraordinary regulation declares that the land underneath residential structures on a farm must be assessed by its agricultural use, not as residential land.

Kansas

Kansas provides preferential tax treatment for agricultural and forest-lands, or lands devoted to timber production. Those preferences are provided via use-value assessment and different assessment ratios. Kansas Statutes Chapter 79—Taxation's Article 14 on Property Valuation, Equalizing Assessments, Appraisers, and Assessment of Property requires that valuations be established for each parcel of real property at fair market value. In addition, those statutes provide that each parcel of land devoted to agricultural use also be valued on the basis of the agricultural income or productivity of the land. The statute specifies that the land be valued "upon the basis of the agricultural income or productivity attributable to the inherent capabilities of such land in its current usage under a degree of management reflecting median production levels" (1).

Starting in 2000, every parcel of real property is required to be actually viewed and inspected by the assessor once every six years. That requirement implies that approximately 17 percent of the parcels must be inspected each year. Agricultural land is classified by soil type and productivity using USDA information for each relatively homogeneous region of the state. An eight-year moving average is used to measure productivity and other characteristics of the land for classification purposes. The International Association of Assessing Officers (IAAO) has commended Kansas for exemplary comprehensiveness and completeness in its use-value methodology, according to the Kansas Department of Revenue (2000). The state director of property valuation is required to make an annual determination of land values for each class of property within each county or homogeneous region and provide that information to the county assessors, who then must use those valuation schedules to classify lands in their counties according to current usage. The director applies the values appropriate to each class.

Commodity prices, crop yields, and pasture and rangeland rental rates and expenses used in determining net income are also computed using an eight-year moving average. Net income for each land classification in each county is then capitalized to determine use value. Kansas has a very odd statute specification for the capitalization rate that should be used to capitalize the net income, however. The statute specifies a number of factors to be summed to derive the capitalization rate, and it then overrides the potential sum by restricting the final rate to a unit interval between 11 and 12 percent. Kansas Statute 70-1476 requires a capitalization rate that is the sum of

> the contract rate of interest on new federal land bank loans in Kansas on July 1 of each year averaged over a five-year period which includes the five years immediately preceding the calendar year which immediately precedes the year of valuation, plus a percentage not less than .75 percent nor more than 2.75 percent, as determined by the director of property valuation, except that the capitalization rate calculated for property tax year 2003, and all such years thereafter, shall not be less than 11 percent nor more than 12 percent. (1)

When local property tax rates are added, this procedure resulted in capitalization rates for 2011 agricultural land assessments ranging from a low of 13.11 percent in Stevens County to a high of 15.66 percent in Russell County.

For pasture or rangeland, the net rental income received from the landlord is used in computing use value. Land enrolled in the USDA Conservation Reserve Program (CRP) is classified as cultivated dry land for tax purposes. Land enrolled in the federal Wetlands Reserve Program is classified as native grassland for tax purposes.

Once use value is determined for agricultural land, Kansas sets the taxable value at 30 percent of the use value. In this way, Kansas provides large reductions in property taxes for agricultural landowners, as it not only values the land in current use, but then reduces that value by 70 percent. The Council of State Governments (2012) reports that other states doing something similar include Illinois (33.33 percent of use value) and South Dakota (85 percent of use value).

Ohio

Ohio provides preferential tax treatment for agricultural land, conservation or open-space lands, and forestlands or timber production lands. Those preferences are provided through current-use valuation. Ohio's program of use-value assessment is known as the Current Agricultural Use Value (CAUV) Program. Farmers must enroll their land in the CAUV Program to be eligible for use-value assessment. Eligibility requirements include a 10-year commitment to maintain the land in agricultural use. The tax benefits of enrollment in CAUV are provided indefinitely, conditional on the land's remaining in agricultural use. If the land is removed from agricultural use, the landowner is required to pay back the tax reduction provided by the program over the previous three years. Assessors are required to maintain records of the full taxable value of the land for this purpose.

Under the CAUV Program, use value is determined by an income capitalization method. Net income is computed as the farm's projected gross income from agricultural production less its projected nonland production costs. Gross income is projected based on an assumed cropping pattern corresponding to the land's soil types. Ohio has 3,080 different soil types that have been collapsed into six prototypical cropping patterns. A five-year moving average of statewide crop yields is applied to the prototypical cropping patterns to estimate yields. A five-year moving average of crop prices is then applied to the yields to obtain estimated revenue. Nonland production costs are estimated and subtracted from the gross revenue estimates to obtain net income. Once again, five-year moving averages for the nonland input costs are utilized, including "seed, fertilizer, fuel oil, grease, repairs, drying fuel, and electricity costs, fuel for trucking, labor charges, and machinery and equipment charges" (Ohio Department of Taxation 2010, 2). Estimates of these costs are provided by the Ohio Farm Management Enterprise Budgets published by the Ohio State University Department of Agricultural, Environmental, and Development Economics.

The net income estimates are then capitalized into land value using a capitalization rate derived from two sources. Ohio uses a mortgage-equity method for computing the capitalization rate. First, the five-year average Farm Credit Services interest rate for a fifteen-year loan amounting to 60 percent of assets is used. Second, an average of the interest rate on the remaining 40 percent of the assets equity for the previous five years is determined. Third, a five-year anticipated future depreciation or appreciation rate is included, and finally, a five-year average of the state property tax rate. The capitalization rate is computed as a weighted average of the first two interest rates (debt and equity rates), with the weights being 0.6 and 0.4, respectively. This method of estimating the capitalization rate assumes a 60/40 division between debt and equity financing for the farm operation, which does not necessarily match any particular farm's capital structure. Furthermore, there is a mismatch between the debt portion of the estimation, which is a forward-looking interest rate anticipated by Farm Credit Services, and the equity portion of the estimation, which uses a backward-looking five-year average of previous interest rates. Beyond that, the inclusion of an anticipated future five-year depreciation or appreciation rate further mixes historical data with future anticipations in the Ohio rate computation.

Virginia

Virginia provides preferential treatment of agricultural and farmland, open space, forestland and timber production by application of current-use valuation. Agricultural land is defined as "real estate devoted to the bona fide production of plants and animals useful to man" (Va. Code Ann. 58.1–3230). An agricultural parcel must be at least five acres to qualify for use-value assessment. The land is then valued on the basis of its productive earning ability, typically using an income capitalization approach. The Virginia procedure is well described and prototypical, so this case is considered in detail.

The Virginia assessment procedure begins by developing a composite or typical farm for each jurisdiction, which may be a city or a county. Census of Agriculture data are the basis for delineating county summaries of the number of farms and acreage under production. For each crop produced, a total number of acres deployed for that purpose is developed. Dividing the total acreage devoted to each crop by the total number of farms in the county results in a ratio that is used to determine what crops will be included in the development of the composite farm. If the ratio is at least one, indicating that on average at least one acre per farm is used to produce that crop, then that crop is included in the construction of the composite farm.

Bruce and Groover (2007) describe the composite farm for Prince Edward County, for example. That county had 395 farms covering 1,430 acres in corn production. Computing the ratio of land devoted to corn production per farm in the county yields 3.6202 (1,430/395), which is rounded up to the nearest integer, 4. Hence, corn production is included in the composite farm for Prince Edward County, with 4 acres allocated to that crop. The Prince Edward County composite farm has a total of 39 acres, with the remaining 35 acres allocated to alfalfa, hay, wheat, and barley using similar computations.

The next step in developing the use-value assessment is to compute budgets for each crop grown on the composite farm. Annual net income per acre is computed for each crop. Virginia Farm Management crop budgets and input cost data are used for this purpose. Annual crop yields are determined, and annual net income budgets are computed. The annual net income figures are then averaged using a seven-year Olympic moving average. The highest and lowest annual net income figures during the past seven years are omitted when computing the mean return. The Olympic averaging process used in Virginia also truncates the data at zero in case of negative returns.

To determine the productive capacity of the land, Virginia uses the land classification scheme outlined in table 4.3. Land in each class is assigned a Virginia Land Capability Class Index, with index values ranging from a low of 0.10 for Class VIII land to a high of 1.50 for Class I land. The reference class of land is Class III. Other classes of land are judged to be more or less productive by reference to Class III land. The Index is used in a cardinal manner, with Class I land considered to be 50 percent more productive than Class III land, for example. A weighted average of the land productivity indices is computed, as illustrated in table 4.4. The weights are the relative quantities of land in Classes I–IV in the county. Using the total crop acreage and total weighted acreage in table 4.4, the Soil Index Factor (SIF) is computed. The SIF is the quotient of the total weighted acreage and the total acreage. In the example provided in the table, SIF = 45,519/40,504 = 1.15. The computed SIF indicates that the land in Prince Edward County is of quality 1.15, or 15 percent more productive than Class III land.

Finally, the Virginia process calculates a single estimate of the net return for the crops grown on the county-specific composite farm. That is done by taking a weighted average of the crop net returns and the composite farm crop acreages. The outcome of that computation is called the estimated net return. Bruce and Groover (2007) provide the result for Prince Edward County, which had an estimated net return of $18.20/acre. That net income value is then capitalized.

The capitalization rate used in Virginia is the sum of an interest rate and property tax rate, with an additional risk factor included for lands with a risk of flooding. Bruce and Groover indicate that the capitalization rate with an additional risk factor incorporated "should only be used when the soil has poor drainage that is not remedied by tilling or drainage ditches or when the land lies in a floodplain" (2007, 6). Table 4.5 provides

TABLE 4.3

Virginia Land Classification

Land Classification	Description	Virginia Land Capability Class Index
Class I	Soils have few limitations that restrict use.	1.50
Class II	Soils have some limitations that reduce the choice of plants or require moderate conservation practices.	1.35
Class III	Soils have severe limitations that reduce the choice of plants or require special conservation practices, or both.	1.00
Class IV	Soils have very severe limitations that restrict the choice of plants, require very careful management, or both.	0.80
Class V	Soils are subject to little or no erosion but have other limitations impractical to remove that limit their use largely to pasture, range, woodland, or wildlife food and cover.	0.60
Class VI	Soils have severe limitations that make them generally unsuited to cultivation and limit their use largely to pasture or range, woodland, or wildlife food and cover.	0.50
Class VII	Soils have very severe limitations that make them unsuited to cultivation and that restrict their use largely to grazing, woodland, or wildlife.	0.30
Class VIII	Soils and landforms have limitations that preclude their use for commercial plant production and restrict their use to recreation, wildlife, water supply, or aesthetic purposes.	0.10

SOURCE: Bruce and Groover (2007).

TABLE 4.4
Virginia Land Productivity and Soil Index Factor Computation

Land Class	Crop Acreage	Productivity Index	Weighted Acreage
I	418	1.50	627
II	21,273	1.35	28,719
III	10,617	1.00	10,617
IV	8,196	0.80	6,557
TOTAL	40,504		46,519

SOURCE: Bruce and Groover (2007), appendix C, p. 24, with corrections by authors.

TABLE 4.5
Virginia Example of Capitalization Rate Computation

Capitalization Rate Component	Value	Source
Interest rate component	0.0761	10-year average of long-term interest rates charged by the various agricultural credit associations serving Virginia
Property tax component	0.0043	10-year average of the effective true tax rates reported by the Virginia Department of Taxation
Rate without risk	0.0805	Sum of above two components
Risk component	0.0040	0.05 times rate without risk (5% addition)
Rate with risk	0.0845	Sum of above two components

SOURCE: Bruce and Groover (2007), appendix C, p. 24.

an example. The interest rate component is taken from a 10-year average of long-term rates charged by agricultural credit associations in Virginia. The property tax rate component is taken from a 10-year average of the effective true tax rates reported by the Virginia Department of Taxation. The sum of those two components is the capitalization rate, unless a flooding risk component is also included.

Following the example for the composite farm, the estimated net income of $18.20 per acre is capitalized using the 0.0805 rate (without flooding risk) to obtain a use value of $226.17 per acre ($18.20/0.0805). If the composite farm is subject to flooding risk, the capitalized value per acre is $215.40 ($18.20/0.0845). Note that in this capitalization computation, the net income estimate in the numerator is the result of a seven-year Olympic moving average, whereas the denominator capitalization rate is the result of a ten-year moving average of the interest rate and property tax rate. This obvious mismatch in time periods is not justifiable.

Virginia's use-value statute specifies that the final authority for assessments is the local commissioner of revenue. Consequently use-value estimates that may be provided by the Virginia Cooperative Extension to counties or cities are sometimes used verbatim and sometimes adjusted by a commissioner on the basis of localized knowledge.

Virginia statutes provide no indication of how to determine the size of the flood risk adjustment. On this issue Bruce and Groover (2007, 6) provide insightful general commentary:

> Agricultural enterprises are subject to numerous risks. However, the risks associated with input costs, crop yields, and prices received are adequately accounted for by the net-return component since these risks occur on an across-the-board basis and do not reflect individual land-risk situations. The two primary types of risks are related to rainfall, either a shortage or an excessive amount. An important difference between the two is that the risk associated with drought *is not* land-related while the risk associated with excessive rainfall *is* land-related. The risk of drought is assumed to be distributed uniformly within a jurisdiction and, therefore, does not warrant special attention. Because the risk associated with an excessive rainfall is land-related, it can vary within a jurisdiction. The risk associated with excessive rainfall is lower crop yields caused by flooding. . . . Because this risk is borne by specific areas of land within a jurisdiction, a special use-value estimate based on a capitalization rate reflecting the risk of flooding is calculated.
>
> The size of the risk component will vary depending on the period over which a total crop loss is expected on lands subject to the effects of flooding. Use-value methodology assumes that a total crop loss will occur once every 20 years. Therefore, the land's capitalization rate is increased by 5 percent.

This commentary makes the important point that most risk elements are automatically incorporated in the numerator of the net income capitalization equation. Parcel-specific risk adjustments may be appropriate, as with the risk of flooding. But a simple 5 percent scaling up of the capitalization rate, based on a 20-year flood assumption, is little more than ad hoc. In practice, assessors should have solid objective data on which to make such adjustments.

Wisconsin

Wisconsin changed in 1995 from reliance on a circuit breaker mechanism that provided property tax relief for agricultural property enrolled in its agricultural nondevelopment program to a use-value regime. The 1995–1997 Budget Act changed the assessment standard from market value to use value. After a transition phase, use-value assessment was fully implemented in the year 2000. The Wisconsin Department of Revenue (2010) statutes specify that agricultural land "shall be assessed according to the income that could be generated from its rental for agricultural use" (2). A Farmland Advisory Council (FAC) is charged with the responsibility of computing per-acre values for agricultural land, based on rental income.

The Wisconsin Department of Revenue (2012) outlines a four-step process for the determination of use-value assessments. First, there must be a determination of the estimated gross income per acre for each county. Second is a determination of the estimated average net income per acre for each county. Third, there must be a determination of the capitalization rate. Finally, there is the estimation of use value using an income capitalization formula.

The determination of the estimated gross income per acre in each county requires calculation of the five-year average base corn yield per acre. County corn yields reported by the Wisconsin Agricultural Statistics Service are the designated measure of land productivity used for estimating average gross income per acre. The assessment manual states, "Annual county corn yields reflect variability in weather, changes in technology, and the prevalent soil conditions in each county" (Wisconsin DOR 2006, 11-B-2). Since reliable corn-yield data are only available at the county level, county average gross income per acre is the base value used in the Wisconsin model. Furthermore, for counties with small acreages of planted corn, estimates are produced based on the yields from nearby counties, with linear extrapolation. A five-year estimated average corn price is then computed based on a 60-month moving average using USDA National Agricultural Statistics Service (NASS) data for Wisconsin. Gross income per acre is derived as the product of yield per acre and price per bushel.

To determine the estimated average net income per acre for each county, the specified procedure is to calculate the landowner's net income per acre under a crop-share lease. A return to management and a cost estimate of production are then subtracted from that gross income to derive net income. Cost data, taken from county-specific USDA published costs, include "cost of seed, fertilizer, soil conditioners, manure, chemicals, custom operations, other variable cash expenses, and interest on operating capital" (Wisconsin DOR 2012, 11-B-5). A management expense of 7.5 percent of gross income is also subtracted. That expense accounts for administrative and land maintenance expenses (such as weed eradication, laser leveling, irrigation ditch construction, and other costs related to maintaining or improving the productivity of the land).

The capitalization rate is determined by adding a five-year average agricultural loan rate and a property tax rate. That sum is then compared to 11 percent, and the larger of the two figures is used to capitalize net income to compute land value. The interest rate is computed as the five-year average of the effective one-year adjustable rate mortgage rates for medium-sized agricultural loans taken from a survey of federal land credit associations (FLCA) and agricultural credit associations (ACA) in Wisconsin. The property tax rate is specified as the "effective full value tax rate" (Wisconsin DOR 2012, 11-B-6).

Wisconsin's requirement to compute the five-year average of the effective rate using one-year adjustable rate mortgage (ARM) rates is unusual. The difference is that Wisconsin's procedure relies on a very short-term (one year) rate. In addition, Wisconsin statutes provide for the rate to be modified based on the stock requirement of the FLCA or ACA providing the loan. Being cooperatively owned by their borrowers, such institutions grant loans that are subject to stock purchase requirements. As a result, Wisconsin requires that the effective interest rate be computed net of the stock purchase requirement. Consider an example where a borrower obtains a $100,000 loan at 9 percent interest and is required to purchase $2,000 in stock. That requirement is a 2 percent stock requirement, resulting in net proceeds of the loan being $98,000. Wisconsin statutes require that the effective interest rate be computed as 9 percent divided by (1-.02), which is equal to 9.18 percent. Note, however, that this computation overstates the effective interest rate because it implicitly assumes that no dividend is paid on the stock.

The final step in estimating use value is to calculate the return for land of grades 2 and 3, as well as the return for pastureland in the jurisdiction. The nine agricultural districts in Wisconsin are grouped into three latitudinal tiers: North, Central, and South. The use value for land of grades 2 and 3 is computed using the relationships between average soil productivity for each grade of soil in each regional tier. Soil productivity ratios (PR) are computed in each tier by taking the ratio of average grade 1 productivity to average grade 2 productivity, and the ratio of average grade 2 productivity to average grade 3 productivity. Using the PR ratios, the five-year average corn yield for grade 1 land in any county can then be used to estimate corn yields for land of grades 2 and 3 in the county. Those estimated corn yields are then used to derive estimated gross income for land of each grade of soil. Net income is then computed by subtracting operating and management expenses.

Annual changes in agricultural use value are also limited in Wisconsin. For each type of agricultural land, increases and decreases in use value are limited to the prior year's percentage change in the statewide equalized value. The rate of growth limit is the annual statewide change in equalized values less the value of agricultural land and new construction.

Having surveyed the empirical evidence on how use-value assessments are calculated in a number of states, this chapter turns to a survey of empirical studies on the impacts of UVA programs after their implementation, including evidence on what factors encourage private landowners to enroll in UVA programs, whether UVA preserves family farms and rural landscapes, what effects UVA has on the distribution of property tax payments among taxpayers, and what effects UVA has on property tax administration.

Enrollment in Use-Value Assessment Programs

Studies of landowner enrollment have focused primarily on California's Williamson Act (CLCA) program. One of the earliest studies of the decision to voluntarily enroll in a use-value assessment program is Hansen and Schwartz (1975). The authors collected assessment and CLCA enrollment data for three study areas near Sacramento, California, as well as attitudinal survey data for landowners in those areas. They report that, "with few exceptions, CLCA parcels in all three areas are located away from development activity. . . . Much smaller average parcel size and acreage per owner for non-enrolled parcels were observed in each study area. . . . This result could be attributed to the greater development potential of these parcels, since parcel sizes were smaller closer to developing areas" (345–346). The authors also report that landowners who were farmers were more likely to enroll in the Williamson Act program than professionals, retirees, and corporations owning rural parcels in the same study areas. Because of the limited geographic scope of this study (Sacramento County) and the long-term contractual commitment required by the CLCA program, one should not generalize these findings to UVA programs in other states.

In a related simulation exercise, Schwartz, Hansen, and Foin (1976) find that changes in the provisions of the CLCA are unlikely to substantially affect the rate of enrollment in California's UVA program. The main exception is that shortening the minimum term of the CLCA contract would encourage more landowners to enroll.

Carman (1977) offers a more comprehensive view of landowner participation in California's Williamson Act program. He collected county-level acreage data on CLCA enrollment from 1967 through 1975 and estimates time-trend equations for 40 participating counties. For most counties, the acreage time trend can be described by a logistic function.[1] The author then correlates two parameters of the county logistic functions

---

1. Marin and Napa counties are two exceptions. Carman speculates that strict agricultural zoning substitutes for CLCA enrollment in that pair of counties (1977, 286).

(upper asymptote and rate of growth of total acreage) with several variables that might explain intercounty differences in enrollment. Carman concludes that

> the rate and level of acceptance of the [Williamson] Act is inversely related to the expected opportunity to convert agricultural land to urban uses at a profit. . . . [Surprisingly,] counties with the largest per acre tax reductions tended, other things being equal, to have lower rates and levels of acceptance of use-value assessment. It is likely that landowners in those counties view nonagricultural development as offering significant opportunities for realizing capital gains. (285–286)

Preservation of Small Family Farms

As noted in chapter 2, a stated goal of UVA advocates has always been a desire to preserve the small family farm in the United States. Has UVA of agricultural land contributed to survival of family farms during recent decades? This question has not been studied extensively, but the available evidence is weak, at best, for this argument in favor of UVA adoption.

According to a survey of farmers reported by the Council on Environmental Quality (1976), a host of considerations enter into the decision of a farm owner to sell his property and leave the land. While an individual farmer's decision is not the focus of UVA concerns, the aggregate effect of large numbers of farmers exiting agriculture is. The after-tax returns from agricultural production certainly play a role, and hence preferential assessment could affect the decisions of some farmers. However, the age of the owner and whether he plans to bequeath the farm to a relative or sell the property to fund his retirement is another consideration. Finally, a farmer on the metropolitan fringe might sell, not because of rising property taxes but because of worsening traffic on rural roads, growing air pollution from urban sources, and neighbors' complaints about farm odors. One implication of this early survey is that detecting the impact of preferential assessment on survival of small farmers requires a degree of econometric sophistication.

Chicoine (1981) documented some of these pressures on farmers to sell with his hedonic model of agricultural land prices on the fringe of metropolitan Chicago. Using data for 1,400 sales of unimproved farmland in Will County, Illinois, from 1970 to 1974, he found that sale price per acre correlated positively and significantly with proximity to downtown Chicago and to the nearest freeway exchange, with suitability of the parcel's soil for a septic system, with residential or industrial/commercial zoning of the parcel, and with the fraction of adjoining acres already developed as commercial or industrial properties. Interestingly, the sale price of an acre did not correlate with its soil productivity index for agricultural purposes. Hence, by the early 1970s, the price of rural land dozens of miles from Chicago's Loop reflected its potential urban uses. Chicoine concludes: "This fact supports urban fringe preferential farmland property tax assessments to discourage the premature removal of land from agriculture" (1981, 360). While that study endorsed the potential use of UVA to preserve agricultural land at the urban fringe, it provided no evidence that UVA would be effective in doing so.

Chicoine, Sonka, and Doty (1982) employ a simulation methodology to examine the effects of circuit breakers and use-value assessment on the financial position of a typical Illinois farmer over a 10-year period. They assume a corn/soybean operation on 600 acres with the operator owning half the acreage and sharecropping the remaining half. They also assume that the only labor input comes from the operator and her family. Employing actual data on crop yields and crop prices to calibrate their model, the authors simulate the annual after-tax income and property tax payments of the operator either with market-value or use-value assessment of the farm property or with a circuit breaker provision.

What is their conclusion? "With both property tax relief programs, the reduction in average annual property taxes is reflected in . . . [higher] after-tax average annual incomes. But the cash situation remains dismal, suggesting that even with property tax relief the operator and landlord would . . . likely have to liquidate part of their land base to continue operations" (520). This simulation exercise suggests that the capacity of UVA programs to preserve family farmers is quite limited.

A limited capacity of UVA programs to keep small farmers in operation would help to explain why farms in the United States are now frequently owned by families with higher levels of income and net worth.

According to Park et al., "Median farm household income increased by 3.7 percent in 2010 to $54,162. . . . Bolstered by higher farm asset values, the balance sheet of farm households improved in 2010, with median net worth increasing by 6.5 percent to $576,745" (2011, 1). Policy makers need to ask whether or not wealthy taxpayers with high incomes deserve substantial tax breaks for owning rural land.

Preservation of Rural Landscapes

A question closely related to the preservation of small family farms is whether use-value assessment has actually helped to preserve rural land that generates environmental amenities and ecosystem services. In an early study of the empirical relationship between property taxation and land use change, the Council on Environmental Quality (1976) correlated percent change in agricultural land, 1969–1973, in a sample of Ohio counties with absolute change in population density, gross cash receipts per farm acre, percent of farmers over 65 years of age, and property tax paid per acre. This rather simplistic study found that a higher property tax per acre was associated with a greater percentage loss of farmland during the period studied. Although this study tried to control for some influences on land use change other than the property tax, its simple methodology did not correct for potential statistical problems such as endogeneity.

Blewett and Lane (1988) used the 1963 introduction of use-value assessment in Indiana to conduct a before-and-after study of the rate of agricultural farmland loss in that state. Using data for 92 counties, they correlated percent decline in farmland acres with the percentage changes in population, property taxes per acre, and number of elderly farmers during two periods, 1954–1959 and 1964–1969. Their statistical results indicate an increase in the negative intercept term after the introduction of preferential assessment of farmland and a change in the coefficient on the property tax variable from a positive and significant one to an insignificant one. These results suggest that the implementation of current-use assessment slowed the conversion of Indiana farmland to urban uses.

Parks and Quimio (1996) focus their empirical study on changes in farmland acreage in New Jersey between 1949 and 1990. This historical period includes the 1964 constitutional amendment that permitted current-use assessment of agricultural land in the Garden State. Using annual state-level data measured in logarithms, the authors correlated agricultural land area with net farm revenue per acre (excluding the property tax), annual percentage changes in the market value of farmland, the interest rate on farm credit, and the effective property tax rate. Although their statistical equation can explain much of the annual variation in agricultural land area and the authors have corrected for autocorrelation, their use of proxies to measure several explanatory variables suggests that their statistical results should be viewed with caution.

That said, they find that the elasticity[2] of agricultural land area with respect to the effective property tax rate is −0.066. This elasticity estimate implies that the cut in the effective property tax rate on agricultural land that followed implementation of UVA had a very modest impact on the conversion rate of farmland after 1964. The authors conclude that New Jersey needs to rely more heavily on its purchase-of-development-rights program in order to protect its remaining farmland from urban development.

In perhaps the only empirical study of use-value assessment of national scope, Morris (1998) used interstate differences in the year that preferential assessment was introduced to measure its cumulative impact on the availability of agricultural land in nearly 3,000 counties across the United States.[3] From 1959 through 1987, the mean percentage of a county's land in farming fell from 63.9 percent to 52.5 percent. The author's empirical question is whether earlier state adopters of preferential assessment had a substantially higher percentage of farmland in their counties at the end of the study period.

Morris correlated the percentage of farmland in a county during a particular year with a series of dummy variables measuring the number

---

2. The elasticity of any variable x with respect to any variable y is defined as the ratio of the percentage change in x to the associated percentage change in y.

3. Forty-seven states introduced use-value assessment between 1957 and 1986, with a peak period of adoption during the late 1960s and early 1970s (Morris 1998, figure 7.1).

of years since adoption of preferential assessment plus county and year fixed effects. The results suggest that after 20 years of use-value assessment, a state's counties would tend to have 10 percentage points more land in farming associated with this tax policy. If one distinguishes between counties with rollback penalties and those with no development penalties, one finds that counties in states with rollback penalties had a significantly greater loss of farmland than those with penalty-free preferential assessment. Morris interprets these results to mean that states adopting deferred tax policies were the ones more prone to lose farmland in the first place.

In an effort to correct for this statistical endogeneity problem, Morris augments her original regression equation with control variables for population density, property tax per capita, value of farm sales per acre, and value of farmland and buildings per acre. The augmented regression implies that "preferential assessment of farmland can indeed delay the conversion of farmland to other uses. The policy produced a gradual but significant difference in the loss of farmland that after a 20-year period amounted to about 10 percent more of the land in a county being retained in farming. ... The results also ... suggest that the policy may be more effective when property tax burdens are higher" (1998, 156).

Brockett, Gottfried, and Evans (2003) ask whether the 1976 enactment of Tennessee's Greenbelt Law was necessary to protect forested land from development. They studied 337 parcels in Franklin County that enjoyed use-value assessment in early 1999. The authors estimate the reservation prices of parcel owners given assessors' valuations, tax savings from enrollment in the Greenbelt program, prospective development penalties, *and* alternative assumptions about the reservation premium of owners, that is, the intangible benefits from ownership of forested parcels.[4] They conclude that, if the reservation premium of owners was zero, then the Greenbelt Law afforded some degree of protection to all parcels. If, on the other hand, the reservation premium was $500 per acre, then 57 percent of the parcels required no protection. This result implies that the ratio of tax expenditure

---

4. The reservation price is the lowest price that an owner would accept in order to induce him or her to sell.

to acres saved from development could be quite high in situations where all owners of rural land are eligible to enroll their properties in a use-value assessment program.

Polyakov and Zhang (2008) offer a study of use-value assessment that is statistically rigorous and rich in empirical detail. After assembling a panel data set describing land uses on more than 13,000 private parcels in Louisiana during four years between 1982 and 1997, they estimate the Markov transition probabilities for these parcels. That is, they observe transitions between agricultural, forestry, and developed uses during various years and try to explain the likelihood of changes in land use. Their hypothesis is that a higher pretax return per acre or a lower property tax per acre associated with a specific use increases the probability that any parcel will be retained in or shifted to that use. The authors use returns and taxes at the parish level to approximate actual returns and taxes at the parcel level of observation.

Their main conclusion is that "the probabilities of land-use transition or retention are relatively inelastic with respect to property taxes" (2008, 405). In other words, the likelihood of land use change as property tax per acre varies does not seem to fluctuate much. More specifically, the authors find that the elasticity of the transition probability from agricultural to developed use, with respect to the property tax per acre in agricultural use, equals 0.0319. The elasticity of the transition probability from forestry to developed use, with respect to the property tax per acre of forestland, is 0.0184.

These small effects do not mean, however, that Louisiana's current-use assessment program has been inconsequential. The authors simulate complete repeal of the program in 1992, an action that would have doubled the property tax per acre of forestland and tripled the property tax per acre of agricultural land. Their simulation suggests that Louisiana would have lost an additional 162,000 acres of farmland by 1997 if repeal had taken place. Interestingly, however, most of that farmland would have transitioned to forestland, and the additional land devoted to urban uses would have been fewer than 6,000 acres.

In his study of California's Williamson Act (CLCA) Program, Kovacs (2009) analyzes county-level data on contract nonrenewals from 2000 through 2007. He is particularly interested in discovering what variables help to explain a transition from a slow to rapid rate of farmland conversion and vice versa. Using a proportional hazards model with fixed effects and random effects, the author finds that more rapid population and income growth hasten the transition to a high rate of removal of farmland from the Williamson Act Program. Proximity to cities, the Pacific Ocean, and major highways also increases the hazard (probability of transition conditional on no transition to date) of transition to a rapid rate of land conversion. Of greater relevance to this work, a 1 percent increase in the property tax rate reduces the hazard of a transition to a high rate of land conversion by nearly a quarter. Kovacs concludes that "differential assessment programs help to reduce urban sprawl and thus provide benefits to taxpayers" (2009, 24).

It seems, then, that while there is mixed evidence, some UVA programs appear to have slowed the rate of land conversion from rural to developed uses. However, we hasten to note that UVA programs cannot permanently prevent land development. At best, they postpone the dates when private landowners will choose to develop their properties.

Shifts of the Property Tax Burden and Equity Issues

Although empirical research has shown that use-value assessment of rural land has slowed the rate of development of rural land in some states, one needs to ask how expensive this land conservation policy has been for taxpayers and who has borne this program cost.

In its 1976 report on preferential assessment of farms and open space, the President's Council on Environmental Quality candidly noted that these state programs result in tax expenditures of significant magnitude that redistribute income among taxpayers:

> All differential assessment laws ... [entail] "tax expenditures," by means of which the tax bills of some taxpayers are reduced. . . . In most cases, the cost of this reduction is spread over all the other taxpayers. . . . The effect of a tax expenditure is precisely the same as if the taxpayers who receive the benefit were to pay taxes at the same rate as other, nonpreferred taxpayers, and then were to receive a simultaneous grant . . .

in the amount of the tax benefit. . . . Tax expenditures for the federal government must be estimated in the annual budget. . . . [R]eal property tax systems are riddled with tax expenditures of significant [but hidden] magnitude. (1976, 6–8)

In an early study of California's CLCA Program, Hansen and Schwartz (1975) gathered assessment and enrollment data for roughly 800 agricultural parcels in three rural areas of Sacramento County. Those public data are augmented by a survey of parcel owners. Although the authors do not report statistical-significance tests, they do report that the average parcel size owned by owners participating in the program was more than three times the average acres owned by nonparticipating owners. This provides some evidence that the tax savings in Sacramento County during the early years of the Williamson Act Program accrued largely to those with large landholdings. This paper also reports that those owners who had enrolled their agricultural land in the CLCA program enjoyed property tax reductions ranging from 37.9 percent for producers of row crops to 80.2 percent for ranchers with dry pasture.

Of course, the number of acres held by an owner says nothing about her total net worth or annual income. In a follow-up study, Hansen and Schwartz (1977) report on the distribution of tax savings enjoyed by individual and subchapter S owners of CLCA agricultural land in Sacramento County. They report that those owners with net taxable family income in the lowest categories received 12.5 percent of net income but 45.2 percent of net CLCA benefits. Hence, it appears in this very specific case that use-value assessment resulted in a progressive distribution of program benefits.

Dunford and Marousek (1981) studied the impact of the 1970 passage of the Open Space Tax Act (OSTA) in Washington State on the distribution of the property tax burden in Spokane County. They employed an algebraic model of the impact of UVA on the aggregate tax base and on the property tax rate hike required to hold total revenue constant.[5]

---

5. Their algebraic formulas do not account for the possibility that the tax savings from preferential assessment could be capitalized into land prices so that purchasers of land already enrolled in the OSTA Program might not gain from the program.

According to the authors, relatively large increases in the taxes on unenrolled properties should be expected in localities with a small total tax base where a large portion of the total tax base is eligible for and enrolled in the UVA program, and where enrolled land receives a large percentage reduction in assessed value.

Eight years after enactment of the OSTA program, roughly 444,000 acres in Spokane County had been enrolled, 40 percent of the county's total land area. Dunford and Marousek calculate that the revenue-neutral increase in property taxes paid by nonparticipating properties to offset the tax cuts enjoyed by owners of enrolled parcels would equal 1.3 percent. Hidden within this countywide average, however, are huge differences among communities. Although the tax shift to nonparticipating properties would be less than 2 percent in many localities, it would range from 0.6 to 21.9 percent. The larger tax shifts would occur in mostly rural communities with a high proportion of the local tax base eligible for OSTA enrollment.

In an interesting study of state and local fiscal interactions, Chicoine and Hendricks (1985) point out that implementation of a UVA program: (1) results in little tax shifting within a locality if it merely formalizes earlier de facto preferential assessment of eligible properties; and (2) can shift a substantial tax burden from local taxpayers to state taxpayers. The authors studied the impact of the 1980 implementation of mandatory use-value assessment of agricultural land in Illinois. Their study area consisted of the three school districts in Coles County, a grain-producing area of the state. They found that informal and formal use-value assessment of farmland lowered assessed value per pupil and qualified these districts for more generous state educational grants distributed by Illinois's district-power-equalizing aid formula. Prior to implementation of use-value assessment, de facto preferential assessment had already garnered an additional $2.8 million of state aid for the county's school districts. Implementation of formal current-use assessment qualified the county for an additional $115,000 of state educational funding. As a result, the interaction between preferential assessment and state aid lowered the local property tax bills of farm and nonfarm owners alike in Coles County.

Hickman and Crowther (1991) report on a study of the property tax shift that occurred in the 43 easternmost counties of Texas because of its use-value assessment program. These counties contain most of the state's commercial timberland, properties that became eligible for preferential assessment in May, 1979. As of 1987, the authors' study year, roughly 9.3 million acres not in timber use and 7.5 million acres in timber use had been enrolled in the state's UVA program. Of these acres that were forested, the average assessment reduction per acre ranged from $5,825 in Harris County (metro Houston) to $277 in Red River County.

Assuming constant property tax rates across the region and no capitalization effects of preferential assessment on aggregate assessments, the authors calculate that UVA would have cost Harris County $301 million in property tax revenue during 1987. Under these assumptions, the average revenue loss for all 43 counties would have exceeded 6.9 percent. Of course, local governments frequently do not freeze their property tax rates when assessed valuations fall. Rather, they raise their tax rates in an effort to mitigate or even prevent cuts in local public spending. The authors calculate that a tax shift of $133 million to ineligible and nonparticipating properties in eastern Texas would have been required in 1987 to fully offset the impact of UVA. This sum amounts to 5.1 percent of actual property tax revenue in that year across the 43 counties.

Anderson and Griffing (2000a) report estimates of the tax expenditures in two Nebraska counties associated with the state's greenbelt UVA program.[6] They gathered county assessor parcel-level data on market value and use value, and then correlated the ratio of use value to market value with distance of the parcel from the nearest urban center, parcel size, and dummies for school districts contained in the county. They find that this parcel value ratio does indeed correlate as expected with distance, size, and school district.

---

6. This article also provides a readable summary of several microeconomic models of land price determinants within a metropolitan region (2000a, 35–40).

According to Anderson and Griffing,

> Since the ratio of use value to market value is equivalent to the ratio of property taxes under the two assessment regimes, we know that the tax expenditure is large near the [central business district] . . . and declines with distance. . . . One minus that ratio gives the proportion of property tax forgone due to use-value assessment. . . . The average ratio is 0.639 for properties in Lancaster County and 0.2477 in Sarpy County. Hence, the average tax expenditure [associated with UVA] is approximately 36 percent of revenue in Lancaster County and 75 percent of revenue in Sarpy County. (2001a, 46)

In the most comprehensive effort to measure the tax expenditure associated with UVA programs across the United States, Heimlich and Anderson (2001) apply a state's average property tax rate to the difference between the market value of the state's rural land and the use value of that land. They then sum these results and conclude that the national tax expenditure on state UVA programs in 1995 equaled $1.07 billion, with $218 million in California alone. Although these findings are impressive, they should be accepted with caution because the authors include Michigan (not a UVA state) in their total and because their estimate appears to be based on the value of all rural land in a state, not just rural parcels actually enrolled in its UVA program.

After having surveyed various studies of the tax shifting and tax expenditures associated with UVA programs, what can be concluded about the equity of those programs? The answer to that question depends upon the normative principle of taxation that one accepts. If one believes that the total net worth of a taxpayer should be the object of taxation, then one might object to sharp cuts in taxation on valuable holdings of rural land. If, on the other hand, one accepts the benefit principle of taxation, then preferential assessment of rural land could be justified since "rural landowners may consume fewer [local] services per dollar value of land owned than residential or commercial landowners in the same taxing area" (Morris 1998, 145). Whether rural landowners do indeed receive fewer services per dollar of land owned is an empirical question that has not been carefully studied in the literature, however.

Impacts of UVA on Property Tax Administration

There are a few studies suggesting that state adoption of UVA programs has had broader impacts on the property tax system as a whole. Bowman and Mikesell (1988) propose that greater assessment uniformity would be a social benefit of moving from a regime of de facto preferential assessment to a formal UVA regime. Using sales data for agricultural parcels in 90 Virginia counties during the early 1980s, the authors calculate the coefficient of dispersion (COD) for agricultural properties within a county.[7] The authors find that the counties participating in the state's UVA program have lower COD values. That is, there is greater assessment uniformity within property classifications in the presence of a formalized program of preferential assessment. Hence, the UVA program implicitly trades off a reduction in the mean rate of taxation for a reduction in the variance in assessments.

In the final empirical study included in this survey, Ervin, Chicoine, and Nolte (1986) consider the possibility that adoption of a UVA program could affect the stability of the property tax revenue stream over time. The use of capitalized net farm income to measure the use value of agricultural land and multiple-year lags in updating the use-value estimates employed for tax assessment purposes could, according to the authors, result in the countercyclical movement of farmland assessments. That is, property taxes owed by farmers could be rising because of higher land value assessments just as their cash net incomes are falling. A simulation based on assessment data for Lafayette County, Missouri, during the late 1970s and early 1980s suggests that this countercyclical behavior actually exists.

Summary and Conclusions

This chapter surveyed the existing empirical evidence on how use-value assessment has been implemented and what its various impacts have been since its enactment. State governments have adopted diverse methods to

---

7. The coefficient of dispersion is the average absolute difference of parcel assessment ratios from the median assessment ratio in the county, expressed as a percentage of the median ratio.

measure the use value of eligible rural properties. Because the measurement techniques in some cases are not well grounded in economic and assessment theory, some changes in use-value measurement practice are recommended in the next chapter.

Evidence on the impacts of UVA programs leads to the following set of conclusions. First, enactment of UVA statutes has not halted a long-term decline in small-scale family farming in the United States, as some of its supporters had hoped. Second, there is some evidence that UVA programs have moderated, but not halted, the expansion of metropolitan regions into the countryside. Third, the capacity of UVA programs to delay development of rural land parcels may be temporary at best and can be expensive. Assessment of rural properties below market values entails a substantial loss of potential property tax revenue and sometimes results in a regressive shift of property tax burden to other properties that are not eligible for UVA enrollment.

5 \ Criticisms and Reform Recommendations

Chapters 1 through 4 described the historical origins, design features, land conservation effects, and economic impacts of use-value assessment (UVA) programs across the United States. For the most part, those chapters have been descriptive and retrospective. Thus far, this book has not emphasized the numerous criticisms that elected officials, journalists, and economists have lodged against the UVA approach to land conservation since its inception. Chapter 5 will detail and evaluate those criticisms, and will propose several policy reforms that could improve the effectiveness and fairness of UVA programs.

Criticisms of UVA Programs

Enrollment of inappropriate properties in UVA programs

As noted earlier, use-value assessment (UVA) enrollment of rural properties with development potential entails a substantial loss of property tax revenue for local governments. This tax expenditure can be justified only if the policy goals of UVA statutes are realized when those rural properties are enrolled. In most states, the legislative intent underpinning UVA programs was a desire to provide financial relief for professional farmers and to preserve arable land, open space, and forests from urban development.

A persistent problem with UVA programs has been that some owners enroll their rural parcels and enjoy the tax benefits of doing so even though they fully intend to develop their acreages in the near future. This lack of a long-term commitment to rural uses of a land parcel can be detected in a number of ways. The owner, for example, may have earned negligible revenues and net income from selling agricultural commodities or forest products during recent years. The owner might also have requested a change in zoning that would permit commercial, industrial, or residential uses of his parcel or filed subdivision plans with local planning officials. Even if site preparation and construction have not yet begun on a "farm" or other rural parcel, either the absence of significant income from its undeveloped use or actions taken to prepare for physical development of the parcel should raise serious concerns about the intentions of the owner.

As noted at the end of chapter 1, New Jersey's legislature and governor attempted to mitigate this problem of "fake farmers" with the enactment of Senate Bill 589 in April, 2013. That legislation raised the threshold for UVA eligibility from $500 to $1,000 of agricultural or horticultural annual gross sales. Although a threshold of $1,000 is far too low to prevent UVA eligibility of "fake farmers," this recent policy change in the Garden State is a move in the right direction. The new law also requires the State Farmland Evaluation Committee to review that minimum gross sales standard every three years. Frequent review of a state's minimum sales or income threshold for UVA eligibility would become especially important if the inflation rate in the United States were to increase from its low level of recent years.

Another way to eliminate "fake farmers" from the UVA eligibility rolls is to look for evidence that they are preparing to develop their property in the near future. In Arizona, for example, state law directs local assessors to disqualify rural parcels if any of the following conditions exist:

- There is a pending application for rezoning that permits nonagricultural uses.
- A subdivision plat has been recorded, especially if the land is divided into lots of one acre or less.
- There has been recent installation of survey stakes or roads, suggesting nonagricultural development.
- Utility services not required for agricultural use are in place.

This approach to verifying UVA eligibility is probably more costly from a local administrative point of view than simply inspecting the owner's federal tax return. However, detecting these recent actions by a land-owner could be a way to disqualify rural properties that are about to be developed.

Still another reason to suspect that some parcels enrolled in UVA programs are ineligible for preferential assessment is that enrollment in some states relies on self-reporting of eligibility by property owners. The absence of supporting documentation filed by applicants or auditing by local officials suggests that some UVA parcels are, in fact, ineligible for tax preferences under current statutes and administrative regulations.

One exception is Jefferson County, Kentucky. The UVA application form that has to be filed with the county's property valuation administrator is extremely simple to fill out. It asks the property owner to provide his or her name and mailing address, the location and parcel ID number of the relevant property, and a declaration of the acreages used for residential purposes and for *active* agricultural or horticultural use. County officials use these acreage declarations to determine whether the property satisfies a ten-acre minimum for farmland or five-acre minimum for horticultural land under state UVA law.

But how does the county assessor know whether the property is presently being *actively* used for agricultural or horticultural purposes? The owner-applicant is required to submit a copy of the most recent Schedule F (Profit or Loss from Farming) that he or she has filed with the Internal Revenue Service. Schedule F requires the federal taxpayer to submit detailed information about farm sales and subsidies, production and interest costs, and depreciation of farm assets. The farmer who files a Schedule F is subject to an IRS audit, and, if inaccurate information has been declared, the federal government will impose penalties and fines on the taxpayer. Requiring attachment of a Schedule F form to a UVA application is a low-cost method that a state or county agency can use to ensure that the applicant is indeed actively engaged in farming. One limitation of this approach, however, is that requiring Schedule F would exclude many owners who rent their land, not engaging in direct agricultural production, but the land may well be actively used in agricultural production. Rental is passive activity, the income from which is reported on Schedule E. Hence, states may want to require both schedules.

Another reason one might worry that some land parcels already enrolled in a UVA program should not receive preferential assessment is that the minimum acreage requirements in most states are quite low. As noted in table 2.1, agricultural parcels as small as three acres are eligible in Louisiana and Maryland. Farm properties as small as five acres are eligible in Idaho, Maine, Massachusetts, North Carolina, and Rhode Island. In an era when many commercial farms occupy hundreds or even thousands of acres, some might find it hard to believe that properties this small are really farms. However, with the growth of organic farming and community sustainable agriculture in recent years, small farms using labor-intensive methods have begun to reappear alongside large-acreage farms that rely heavily on machinery and chemical inputs. Hence, we do not favor increases in minimum farm size as a requirement for UVA eligibility. To do so could impose a competitive disadvantage on a new generation of "small farmers." Requiring these small farms to generate a substantial amount of revenue from producing and selling farm products is, however, eminently reasonable.

State methods of UVA estimation, including income measurement and discount rate choice

When considering the practical aspects of estimating the current-use value for a property, it is important to start with the fundamental recommendation that the measurement of net income used in the UVA capitalization formula accurately reflects the earning ability of the property. That means it is necessary to estimate the current-use value based on the subject property's actual current use, not a hypothetical prototype's earning ability, as is done in a number of states. An accurate estimate also requires that crop insurance payments, agricultural subsidies, set-aside payments, and other forms of income directly related to the current use of the property be included in the net income measurement. Furthermore, if agricultural land generates joint products such as a cash crop and animal grazing income, both sources of income should be included in the net income measurement. If a joint product such as recreation or hunting generates additional income on rural or agricultural land, those sources of income should also be included in the net income measure.

Choice of a discount rate used in the capitalization formula should ultimately reflect the opportunity cost of capital and include the effective property tax rate. States that have a statutorily fixed rate that is invariant over time should move to a rate reflecting current and anticipated economic conditions. It is also important that states not purposely overestimate or inflate the capitalization rate in order to artificially and arbitrarily lower UVA. Furthermore, states should not impose maximum or minimum limits on the capitalization rate.

If moving averages of net income (in the numerator) and discount rates (in the denominator) are used in estimating UVA, they should be consistent and reflect the same time periods. For example, if the numerator measure of net income is a five-year moving average, the denominator capitalization rate should also reflect a similar time period. If trimmed averages are used for the estimate of net income in the numerator of the capitalization formula, as with so-called Olympic averages, in order to smooth fluctuations over time, they should be symmetric, that is, omit both high and low values. States should not omit just the high value over a given time period, which systematically biases the measurement of use value.

Inadequate penalty provisions in UVA statutes

Another criticism of UVA programs is that many states have failed to design their programs in a way that actually encourages owners of eligible rural parcels to postpone conversion of their land to urban uses. With the exception of a few states like California, private landowners are free to develop their properties at any time if they are willing to make higher property tax payments when their land value assessments increase sharply. Owners who have enrolled their undeveloped land in a UVA program will actually delay development only if they face a properly designed development penalty when their land no longer qualifies for use-value assessment (England and Mohr 2003, 2006). In the absence of a development penalty,

most landowners will simply pocket the tax savings from UVA enrollment and develop their land just as soon as they would have done if UVA
did not exist at all.

If a development penalty is imposed when a rural parcel no longer
qualifies for UVA, that penalty will have a weak effect on the timing of
development if it consists of just a few years of tax savings from past UVA
enrollment. A landowner is likely to keep his property in a UVA program
for a decade or more only if there is a heavy development penalty during the
early years of UVA enrollment and that penalty becomes smaller during
later years. A penalty with these design features is more likely to induce a
landowner to wait a substantial number of years before giving in to development pressures.

Unfortunately, very few states have well-designed development penalties that reward landowners for postponing land use change for a substantial number of years. As appendix 2.3 and table 2.3 document, there are 21
states in which some or all land withdrawn from UVA programs is subject
to no development penalty at all. As a result, eligible landowners in Arizona, Florida, and another 19 states pay an effective property tax rate far
lower than homeowners while their parcels enjoy use-value assessment,
but they are under no financial pressure to delay development of their
properties.

Turning to those states that do levy penalties on properties withdrawn
from UVA programs, in some cases those penalties are likely to have a
very weak impact on the timing of development. In other cases, the penalties have been designed to have a significant impact on when land use
is converted. Returning to table 2.4, Alabama, Minnesota, Illinois, Ohio,
Texas, and Tennessee collect only three years of deferred (rollback) taxes.
This penalty is so modest that it is unlikely to stop a farmer or rancher
from selling his land when a commercial developer or homebuilder comes
calling with an offer.

Other states, however, have enacted UVA development penalties that
are likely to induce landowners to keep their properties enrolled for longer
periods of time. As table 2.4 shows, Delaware, Idaho, and Indiana collect
up to 10 years of deferred taxes when properties lose their eligibility for
use-value assessment. Rhode Island and Vermont are the prime examples

of states with well-designed deterrents to rural land development. In the Ocean State, the penalty is 10 percent of market value during the first six years of UVA enrollment, falling slowly to zero after sixteen years. Although this penalty design cannot prevent eventual development of agricultural or forested land in Rhode Island, it does encourage an owner to defer development for a decade or more. In Vermont, the owner pays a penalty equal to 20 percent of market value if a property has been enrolled for less than a decade. After ten years, the tax rate falls to 10 percent of market value. Once again, the penalty design encourages longer-term UVA enrollment.

One way to strengthen the development penalty feature of a UVA program is to require the landowner to commit to a lengthy enrollment period when her land parcel joins the program and receives a preferential tax assessment. In both California and Georgia, the landowner signs a contract or covenant at the time of program enrollment promising to defer development of her property for at least a decade. Although this contractual obligation encourages the landowner to defer development, it also discourages her from enrolling in the UVA program in the first place (Schwartz, Hansen, and Foin 1975).

Shifting property tax burdens, including efficiency effects and equity considerations

Land taxation is a very efficient form of taxation, generating little or no distortion in the land market and the broader economy. See Dye and England (2009) on the efficiency aspects of the land value tax in particular. Hence, state and local governments relying on the property tax in primarily agricultural or rural areas should be reluctant to move away from property taxation that includes valuation of land based on market values. Compared to other forms of taxation (income, sales, excises, etc.), land taxation is preferable on efficiency grounds. Hence, state and local governments should view with skepticism calls to reduce property taxes on land and raise other forms of taxation.

Current market values reflecting the highest and best use of the land are also the fairest way to implement a property tax. Market values exceed agricultural use values in urbanized areas, but the difference between the two values diminishes with distance from the urban fringe. In predominantly agricultural or rural areas, the difference between market value and use value is minimal. Hence, policy makers should not adopt UVA in predominantly rural areas expecting a reduction in property taxes for rural landowners. UVA artificially values the land and distorts land use decisions. For some policy purposes, that distortion is desired. Indeed, the fundamental reason for UVA application is to distort the market. That being said, however, governments should apply UVA judiciously to situations where it is likely to have the desired effects, not in a blanket fashion to broad classes of property.

UVA programs may be used to shift property tax burdens from agricultural and rural landowners to residential, commercial, and industrial landowners. If the tax burden is shifted to residential property owners, however, especially in a housing market that includes a large number of relatively low-income homeowners, the incidence of UVA will be regressive.

Evidence on the effectiveness of UVA in delaying development or preserving prime agricultural land is mixed. Hence, policy makers should understand that development pressure might well overcome the tax preference provided by UVA in influencing landowners' development decisions. To the extent UVA is effective, the result may only be a temporary delay of development. Other methods of altering land use such as conservation easements, public acquisition, and purchase of development rights programs may be considered for more permanent changes in land use.

If state or local governments wish to address equity concerns, property tax relief measures other than UVA should be considered. Classification of the property tax system is one option, with a whole class of property given a preferential tax rate. This form of tax relief is a blunt policy instrument, however, because it provides tax relief to the entire class of property. A property tax circuit breaker can be considered as an alternative, with relief provided to owners whose property tax is high relative to income. Bowman, Kenyon, Langley, and Paquin (2009) address the use and application of circuit-breaker mechanisms to provide property tax relief.

High cost of achieving UVA policy goals

If preservation of rural landscapes and protection of family farmers are the primary policy goals of UVA programs, then the pursuit of those goals has been very costly to taxpayers and the economy. As Ladd (1980) observed decades ago, "use-value assessment . . . is a blunt policy that benefits all eligible landowners in return for a small supply response at the margin" (19). In plain English, a large tax expenditure is required to protect a limited number of acres from development during any particular fiscal year. Ladd argues that strategic purchases of development rights and even outright public acquisition of rural parcels would be superior tools of public policy with which to influence land use patterns.

Heimlich and Anderson (2001) estimate that the total tax expenditure attributable to UVA programs in 48 states totaled $1.07 billion in 1995. Taking the present value of this annual tax subsidy at a 4 percent discount rate, they find that its long-term value exceeds $26.7 billion. In the long run, however, even this massive subsidy cannot guarantee the permanent protection of a single acre of rural land, no matter how valuable to society.

First Principles for a Rational UVA Program

In light of these criticisms, it is time to reconsider the original intellectual foundation supporting UVA statutes and to find a more compelling and contemporary rationale for the retention of UVA programs. Taking the first step toward a new rationale, consider the following hypothetical example. Imagine two parcels of undeveloped land in New Hampshire that have been enrolled in the state's current-use assessment program. One is a barren acreage that is unsuitable for either commercial agriculture or tree growth. It is, however, a desirable site for warehouse or factory construction because of its proximity to an interstate highway leading to Boston. The other parcel is of equal size, farther north, and also privately owned. Its acreage is thickly forested with white pine trees and is adjacent to the White Mountain National Forest. From a development perspective, this property is not so desirable because of its topography and its lack of highway access.

Which of these parcels is more valuable from an ecological perspective, and which will receive the larger tax break because of use-value assessment? As table 5.1 summarizes, the barren parcel is enrolled in the current-use program as "unproductive" land, and its assessment under New Hampshire law is only $10 per acre. However, with its immediate access to the regional and national highway network, this parcel has a high market value because of its potential use as an industrial site. Hence, UVA enrollment saves the owner of the barren land a great deal of money until industrial development takes place. This parcel is not, however, of any particular ecological significance to society as a whole.[1]

The other parcel, however, is of substantial ecological value. Because it is tree-covered and adjacent to a national forest, its current use helps to extend the habitats of numerous wildlife populations. Its unbroken forest cover enhances the scenic views at a nearby alpine ski resort. The tall pines that crowd its slopes sequester a substantial amount of carbon and also prevent soil erosion and flooding of downhill properties during the spring thaw and snow melt.

TABLE 5.1
Hypothetical Example of Use-Value Assessment

100 acres of unproductive (barren) land
    at interstate highway ramp one hour north of Boston
Assessed Use Value: $1,000
Market Value: $2,000,000

100 acres of white pine forest
    adjacent to White Mountain National Forest and not on a road
Assessed Use Value: $15,000
Market Value: $20,000

1. Although this example is hypothetical, it is based upon the actual assessments of forested and barren land under New Hampshire's current-use program. For up-to-date assessments of various categories of rural land that qualify for UVA enrollment, visit the NH Department of Revenue Administration website and navigate to Current Use Board. In 2013–2014, "unproductive land" was assessed at only $10 per acre. Hence, undeveloped land with valuable development potential could be enrolled in the state's UVA program almost tax-free.

These are some of the valuable ecosystem services provided by the un-developed property, but since the owner cannot charge nearby residents or society at large for these ecological services, they do not enhance the market value of this private property. In fact, because of the remoteness and topography of the parcel, its assessed use value of $150 per acre is only slightly below its market value of $200 per acre. This hypothetical example suggests that current UVA statutes may be effective at briefly delaying the development of properties with highly valuable urban uses but not so effective at identifying and permanently protecting ecologically valuable properties. In this case, wouldn't it be preferable for the federal government to purchase the forested parcel while its market price is low and for local officials to grant the permits necessary for construction of an Amazon warehouse on the barren property? Why should local homeowners and owners of commercial and industrial properties pay higher property taxes to delay the conversion of barren land to its market-determined use as indicated by the real estate market?

The point of this example is that competitive markets normally do a pretty good job of allocating labor, capital, energy—and land—to their "highest and best uses." A number of eminent economists have received the Prize in Economic Sciences in Memory of Alfred Nobel for their studies of the specific conditions under which a system of competitive markets will allocate society's scarce resources with maximum efficiency.[2] Of course, the messiness and complexity of the real world sometimes fail to match the simplicity of economic theories. In other words, under certain conditions, markets will fail to allocate resources efficiently, and corrective public policies (including UVA) might be needed.

Two types of market failure that are relevant to a reconsideration of UVA are externalities and public goods. An example of the former is the impact on water quality if owners of forested parcels adjoining a river were free to clear-cut their properties and chose to do so. Sport fishing and municipal water supplies downstream could be adversely affected by the

---

2. Kenneth Arrow in 1972 and Maurice Allais in 1988 are two examples of Nobel economists who theorized about the power of competitive market forces to allocate resources efficiently—under certain ideal conditions.

private profit calculations of the woodlot owners. However, the "negative externalities" of each logging operation would not be reflected in the market price and profit that each log would generate for its owner. Some examples of "public goods" generated by rural land use are the flood protection and climate moderation that residents of a metropolitan region would enjoy if the surrounding forests remained forested. These important impacts of rural land use that market prices fail to capture are sometimes known as ecosystem services (table 5.2; Boyd and Banzhaf 2006).

A starting point for identifying those rural parcels that deserve UVA eligibility would be the following inequality:

$$U_D < U_R + ESS, \tag{1}$$

where U_D is the current market value of a land parcel in its "highest and best" urban use, U_R is the market value of a land parcel in its "highest and best" rural use, and ESS is the value of the undeveloped parcel as a source of ecosystem services.[3] If a rural land parcel produces livestock, crops, or timber and if it also produces a variety of ecosystem services, then it might deserve to remain undeveloped even if its market value in urban use exceeds its market value in rural use. Use-value assessment could be one policy instrument that would persuade the rural landowner to continue pro-

TABLE 5.2
Ecosystem Services Produced by Rural Landscapes

Pollination by wild insect and bird populations
Support for predator populations that impede disease transmission
Formation of soil from organic material
Storage and filtration of groundwater
Scenic land cover
Protection of aquifers
Maintenance of biodiversity

SOURCE: Boyd and Banzhaf (2006, table 1).

3. Professor Wallace Oates proposed this insight at a Lincoln Institute of Land Policy symposium on UVA, January 14, 2011.

ducing an ensemble of valuable private and public goods.[4] Note, however, that if a land parcel yielded no ecosystem services, then its continued rural use would be hard to justify if its market value in urban use exceeded its market value in rural use. In other words, not all rural land parcels deserve to receive low assessments so that their owners pay low property taxes.

Recommended Reforms of State UVA Programs

Reform of ongoing public policies is never a simple matter because changes in policy almost inevitably create winners and losers within the electorate. Despite that political challenge, reform of UVA programs should be on the political agenda of governors and state legislators. As noted in chapter 1, the property tax remains a crucial source of revenue for local governments in the United States. As documented in chapters 2 through 4, the widespread adoption of UVA programs several decades ago has altered the operation of the property tax in important ways. Existing UVA statutes and administrative rules are imperfect for a number of reasons. These reforms suggested for consideration by citizens and elected officials range from relatively modest and incremental changes in existing law to a major restructuring of use-value assessment programs.

Reform the UVA application process and eligibility requirements

Each property owner should be required to file an annual application for renewal of UVA eligibility. As part of this application, the owner should provide documentary evidence that the property has generated a substantial amount of revenue during the previous year from sale of agricultural, horticultural, or forest products. Because legitimate farms and other rural

---

4. A farm in Tennessee covered by cornfields and woodlots, for example, produces marketable corn while producing nonmarketed services such as wildlife habitat, pollination services, scenic views, carbon sequestration, and groundwater storage. The farmer might be inclined to consider only the revenues and costs associated with corn production, but UVA might nudge her or him in the direction of continuing to produce the ecosystem services for which the market offers no compensation.

enterprises lose money during some years, a minimum revenue test for continued eligibility is preferable to a minimum net income criterion.

The application form should include a checklist of conditions that would reveal intent of the owner to develop his or her property in the near future. This list would include existing zoning for an urban use, a pending application to rezone the parcel for an urban use, recording of a subdivision plan, or installation of streets or utilities not required for rural use. The presence of any of these conditions should disqualify the land parcel for UVA eligibility. Failure to declare any of these conditions on the application form should result in a serious fine levied on the owner. These fines and application fees should fund administrative review of UVA applications and random on-site inspections of enrolled parcels to verify their eligibility.

Adopt a properly designed development penalty

A UVA program without development penalties is bad public policy. Such a program confers property tax breaks on (often wealthy) rural landowners but does nothing to deter development of their properties. Some of those states that did incorporate development penalties in their original statutes adopted extremely weak provisions, and those need to be amended.

Every state should enact a development penalty with a strong deterrent effect. In those states with a rollback penalty, the owners of properties that no longer qualify for UVA should be required to pay the tax savings during all years of enrollment (plus a commercial rate of interest on those savings), up to a maximum of 12 years. In states that impose a land use change tax on the market value of the property when it is developed, it seems reasonable to levy a tax rate of 20 percent during the first decade of enrollment and 10 percent thereafter.

Adoption of use-value estimation methods that are consistent with economic and financial principles

Appropriate application of UVA requires accurate estimation of property value in its current use rather than its current market value. Under a market value standard, the current market value reflects the best possible land use. Under UVA, the assessor must ignore all other potential uses of the property and value it in its current rural or agricultural use. If comparable sales data are used to estimate value, the influence of alternative land uses may well influence the sales prices. As a result, most states specify that under a UVA program, an income capitalization approach be used. Proper use of an income approach requires accurate income data and the choice of a relevant discount rate, as indicated in chapters 3 and 4. A measure of net income earned by the property in its current use is divided by a measure of the opportunity cost of capital, an interest rate called the "discount rate," to obtain an estimate of the property's use value. Hence, proper application of UVA methods using the income approach requires both accurate income measurement and appropriate choice of the discount rate.

The measurement of income must reflect current and expected net income, that is, gross income net of the cost of production. To do this, a time frame must be chosen over which to analyze gross income, production cost, and the opportunity cost of capital. Conceptually, by using a moving average over time, long-term measures of these entities can be used to more accurately estimate use value. Due to annual fluctuations in commodity prices, input prices, and interest rates, a longer time frame is appropriate. There is no single answer to the question of how many years should be used in the moving averages of these measures. Many states use a five- or ten-year moving average, both of which are reasonable. If a shorter time frame is used, the moving averages of commodity prices, input prices, and interest rates will be closer to current values and value assessments will be more volatile, reflecting short-term fluctuations in market conditions. The choice of a longer time frame attenuates moving-average measures and stabilizes use-value estimates of property values.

Whatever time frame is chosen, it is essential that moving averages for all three measures (commodity prices, input prices, and interest rates) be consistent in two ways. First, the time frames must match. If a five-year moving average is used for commodity prices, then the same five-year averaging process should be used for estimates of input prices and interest rates. Second, all three measures must be consistent in their treatment of inflation. If nominal measures of gross income and input costs are used in the numerator, which includes the effects of inflation, then a nominal measure of the discount rate must be used in the denominator. Inflation treatments must be consistent across all measures used in the UVA income approach. Consistency in measurement of both net income and the discount rate is essential for accurate UVA application.

The choice of a discount rate is both very important and difficult, as it must accurately reflect the opportunity cost of capital. Table 4.1 reveals that states use many approaches in selecting or constraining the discount rate. While some methods used by the states are reasonable, others are inappropriate. Appropriate discount rates reflect the current and anticipated opportunity cost of capital, that is, the value of the next best alternative. The choice of discount rate must fundamentally reflect the return to capital with similar risk.

If the income stream is measured in nominal terms, the discount rate should include a risk-free rate and an expected rate of inflation that covers the same time frame. Any further adjustments that add default risk, liquidity, or maturity risk premiums must accurately reflect the opportunity cost of capital with similar risk without artificially inflating the discount rate.

States should not constrain the choice of the discount rate by placing a minimum or maximum value in the statute. The discount rate must reflect the current and anticipated opportunity cost of capital in capital markets that are not static or constrained. Most often, when a state constrains the choice of a discount rate, it specifies a minimum value that is large by historic standards in order to systematically bias the UVA measure downward. This is inappropriate and violates the underlying principles of UVA.

The discount rate must also include a measure of the effective property tax rate that applies to rural and agricultural property. Care should be taken to ensure that the tax rate is an effective rate, not a nominal one (see equation (3) in chapter 3). That is, the effective tax rate must reflect both the assessment ratio and the nominal tax rate. The use of a nominal tax rate that exceeds the effective tax rate has the effect of systematically biasing UVA estimates downward.

Restructure UVA programs to focus eligibility on ecologically valuable parcels

Although a fundamental restructuring of UVA programs might be difficult to achieve politically, citizens and state officials should consider adopting a more targeted approach to preserving rural lands from urban development. This approach would require the applicant to demonstrate that preferential assessment of his or her rural parcel would result in the production of a significant amount of ecosystem services benefiting society as a whole. Undeveloped land would no longer be eligible per se for enrollment in a UVA program. Designing the eligibility criteria to implement this new approach would require the participation of a wide range of experts, including hydrologists, soil scientists, wildlife and forestry managers, climate scientists, and resource economists.

In the final analysis, we need to strive for the proper balance between urban and rural uses of our land. Much of our rural landscape ought to be preserved because of its high ecological value. Other portions of our landscape, however, need to be available for construction of affordable housing, commercial properties, and even industrial facilities. For those rural parcels that await development (and appropriately so), there is no reason to provide their owners with property tax breaks.

References

Alig, Ralph J., Andrew J. Pantinga, SoEun Ahn, and Jeffrey D. Kline. 2003. *Land Use Changes Involving Forestry in the United States: 1952 to 1997, with Projections to 2050.* Gen. Tech. Report PNW-GTR-587. Portland, OR: U.S. Forest Service, Pacific Northwest Research Station.

Anderson, John E. 1986. "Property Taxes and the Timing of Urban Land Development." *Regional Science and Urban Economics* 16(4) (November):483–492.

———. 1993a. "State Tax Credits and Land Use: Policy Analysis of Circuit Breaker Effects." *Resource and Energy Economics* 15(3) (September):295–312.

———. 1993b. "Use-Value Property Tax Assessment: Effects on Land Development." *Land Economics* 69(3) (August):263–269.

———. 2012. "Agricultural Use-Value Property Tax Assessment: Estimation and Policy Issues." *Public Budgeting & Finance* 32(4) (Winter):71–94.

Anderson, John E., and Marlon F. Griffing. 2000a. "Measuring Use-Value Assessment Tax Expenditures." *Assessment Journal* (January/February):35–47.

———. 2000b. "Use-Value Assessment Tax Expenditures in Urban Areas." *Journal of Urban Economics* 48(3) (November):443–452.

Atkinson, Glen W. 1977. "The Effectiveness of Differential Assessment of Agricultural and Open Space Land." *American Journal of Economics and Sociology* 36(2) (April):197–204.

Barlowe, Raleigh. 1978. *Land Resource Economics.* 3rd ed. Englewood Cliffs, NJ: Prentice Hall.

Barlowe, Raleigh, James G. Ahl, and Gordon Bachman. 1973. "Use-Value Legislation in the United States." *Land Economics* 49(2) (May):206–212.

Barnett, Jeffrey L., and Phillip M. Vidal. 2013. "State and Local Government Finances Summary: 2011." Governments Division Briefs. Washington, DC: United States Census Bureau.

Berry, David, and Thomas Plaut. 1978. "Retaining Agricultural Activities Under Urban Pressure: A Review of Land Use Conflicts and Policies." *Policy Sciences* 9(2) (April):153–178.

Bills, Nelson. 2007. "Fifty Years of Farmland Protection Legislation in the Northeast: Persistent Issues and Emergent Research Opportunities." *Agricultural and Resource Economics Review* 36(2) (October):165–173.

Blase, Melvin G., and William J. Staub. 1971. "Real Property Taxes in the Rural-Urban Fringe." *Land Economics* 47(2) (May):168–174.

Blewett, Robert A., and Julia I. Lane. 1988. "Development Rights and the Differential Assessment of Agricultural Land: Fractional Valuation of Farmland is Ineffective for Preserving Open Space and Subsidizes Speculation." *American Journal of Economics and Sociology* 47(2) (April):195–205.

Boldt, Rebecca. 2002. *Impact of Use Valuation on Agricultural Land Values and Property Taxes.* Madison, WI: Wisconsin Department of Revenue, Division of Research and Policy (October).

Bowman, John H. Joseph Cordes, and Lori Metcalf. 2009. "Preferential Tax Treatment of Property Used for Social Purposes: Fiscal Impacts and Public Policy Implications." In *Erosion of the Property Tax Base: Trends, Causes, and Consequences,* ed. Nancy Y. Augustine, Michael E. Bell, David Brunori, and Joan M. Youngman, 269–294. Cambridge, MA: Lincoln Institute of Land Policy.

Bowman, John H., Daphne A. Kenyon, Adam Langley, and Bethany P. Paquin. 2009. *Property Tax Circuit Breakers: Fair and Cost-Effective Relief for Taxpayers.* Policy Focus Report. Cambridge, MA: Lincoln Institute of Land Policy.

Bowman, John H., and John L. Mikesell. 1988. "Uniform Assessment of Agricultural Property for Taxation: Improvements from System Reform." *Land Economics* 64(1) (February):28–36.

Boyd, James, and Spencer Banzhaf. 2006. "What Are Ecosystem Services? The Need for Standardized Environmental Accounting Units." Resources for the Future Discussion Paper 06-02. www.rff.org/Documents/RFF-DP-06-02.pdf.

Brigham, John. 1980. "The Politics of Tax Preference." In *Property Tax Preferences for Agricultural Land,* ed. Neal A. Roberts and H. James Brown, chap. 5. Montclair, NJ: Allanheld, Osmun, and Co.

Brockett, Charles D., Robert R. Gottfried, and Jonathan P. Evans. 2003. "The Use of State Tax Incentives to Promote Forest Preservation on Private Lands in Tennessee: An Evaluation of Their Equity and Effectiveness Impacts." *Politics and Policy* 31(2) (June):252–281.

Bruce, Franklin A., and Gordon E. Groover. 2007. "Methods and Procedures: Determining the Use Value of Agricultural and Horticultural Land in Virginia." Blacksburg, VA: Virginia Cooperative Extension Service, Virginia Tech University.

Bunnell, Gene. 1996. "Implementing Use Value Assessment—A Simple Idea Becomes Complicated." *Perspectives on Planning* 2(2):1–4. Madison, WI: Department of Urban and Regional Planning, University of Wisconsin—Madison/Extension.

California Department of Conservation. 2010. *2010 Williamson Act Status Report.* http://www.conservation.ca.gov/dlrp/lca/stats_reports/Pages/index.aspx.

Capozza, Dennis R., and Robert W. Helsley. 1989. "The Fundamentals of Land Prices and Urban Growth." *Journal of Urban Economics* 26(3) (November):295–306.

Carman, Hoy F. 1977. "California Landowners' Adoption of a Use-Value Assessment Program." *Land Economics* 53(3) (August):275–287.

Chicoine, David L. 1981. "Farmland Values at the Urban Fringe: An Analysis of Sales Prices." *Land Economics* 57(3) (August):353–362.

Chicoine, David L., and A. Donald Hendricks. 1985. "Evidence on Farm Use Value Assessment, Tax Shifts, and State School Aid." *American Journal of Agricultural Economics* 67(2) (May):266–270.

Chicoine, David L., Steven T. Sonka, and Robert D. Doty. 1982. "The Effects of Farm Property Tax Relief Programs on Farm Financial Condition." *Land Economics* 58(4) (November):516–523.

Coe, Richard D. 2009. "The Legal Framework in the United States." In *Land Value Taxation: Theory, Evidence, and Practice*, ed. Richard F. Dye and Richard W. England, chap. 7. Cambridge, MA: Lincoln Institute of Land Policy.

Combs, Susan. 2013. *Tax Exemptions & Tax Incidence: A Report to the Governor and the 83rd Texas Legislature*. Texas Comptroller of Public Accounts. www.window .state.tx.us/taxinfo/incidence/incidence13/96-463_Tax_Incidence2013.pdf.

Conklin, Howard E., and William G. Lesher. 1977. "Farm-Value Assessment as a Means for Reducing Premature and Excessive Agricultural Disinvestment in Urban Fringes." *American Journal of Agricultural Economics* 59(4) (November):755–759.

Coughlin, Robert E., David Berry, and Thomas Plaut. 1978. "Differential Assessment of Real Property as an Incentive to Open Space Preservation and Farmland Retention." *National Tax Journal* 31(2) (June):165–179.

Council of State Governments. 2012. "The Hows and Whys of Taxing Agricultural Land: State Systems Continue to Evolve." http://knowledgecenter.csg.org/drupal /content/hows-and-whys-taxing-agricultural-land-state-systems-continue -evolve.

Council on Environmental Quality. 1976. *Untaxing Open Space: An Evaluation of the Effectiveness of Differential Assessment of Farms and Open Space*. Washington, DC: U.S. Government Printing Office.

Dunford, Richard W., and Douglas C. Marousek. 1981. "Sub-County Property Tax Shifts Attributable to Use-Value Assessments on Farmland." *Land Economics* 57(2) (May):221–229.

Dye, Richard F., and Richard W. England, eds. 2009. *Land Value Taxation: Theory, Evidence, and Practice*. Cambridge, MA: Lincoln Institute of Land Policy.

England, Richard W., and Robert D. Mohr. 2003. "Land Development and Current Use Assessment: A Theoretical Note." *Agricultural and Resource Economics Review* 32(1) (April):46–52.

———. 2006. "Land Development and Current Use Assessment." In *Economics and Contemporary Land Use Policy: Development and Conservation at the Rural-Urban Fringe*, ed. S. K. Swallow and R. J. Johnston, chap. 8. Washington, DC: Resources for the Future.

Ervin, David E., David L. Chicoine, and Paul D. Nolte. 1986. "Use Value Assessment of Farmland: Implications for Fiscal Stability." *North Central Journal of Agricultural Economics* 8(1) (January):17–28.

Fischel, William A. 1982. "The Urbanization of Agricultural Lands: A Review of the National Agricultural Lands Study." *Land Economics* 58(2) (May):236–259.

Forstall, Richard L. 1995. *Maryland: Population of Counties by Decennial Census: 1900 to 1990.* http://www.census.gov/population/cencounts/md190090.txt.

Gardner, B. Delworth. 1977. "The Economics of Agricultural Land Preservation." *American Journal of Agricultural Economics* 59(5) (December):1027–1036.

Gloudemans, Robert J. 1974. *Use-Value Farmland Assessments: Theory, Practice, and Impact.* Chicago: International Association of Assessing Officers.

Hansen, David E., and S. I. Schwartz. 1975. "Landowner Behavior at the Rural-Urban Fringe in Response to Preferential Property Taxation." *Land Economics* 51(4) (November):341–354.

———. 1977. "Income Distributional Effects of the California Land Conservation Act." *American Journal of Agricultural Economics* 59(2) (May):294–301.

Heimlich, Ralph E., and William D. Anderson. 2001. *Development at the Urban Fringe and Beyond: Impacts on Agriculture and Rural Land.* Agricultural Economic Report No. 803, USDA Economic Research Service.

Hickman, Clifford A., and Kevin D. Crowther. 1991. *Economic Impacts of Current-Use Assessment of Rural Land in the East Texas Pineywoods Region.* Research Report SO-261, U.S. Forest Service, Southern Forest Experimental Station.

Indiana Department of Local Government Finance. 2013. "Certification of Agricultural Land Base Rate Value for Assessment Year 2012." http://www.in.gov/dlgf/files/111230_-_Certification_Letter_-_2012_Agricultural_Land_Base_Rate.pdf.

International Association of Assessing Officers (IAAO). 2008. "Standard on Mass Appraisal of Real Property." Kansas City, MO: International Association of Assessing Officers.

Iowa Department of Revenue. 2008. *Iowa Real Property Appraisal Manual.* www.iowa.gov/tax/locgov/propmanual.html.

Kansas Department of Revenue. 2000. Kansas Statutes Annotated. 79-1476, Chapter 79—Taxation, Article 14—Property Valuation, Equalizing Assessments, Appraisers and Assessment of Property. http://kansasstatutes.lesterama.org/Chapter_79/Article_14/.

Keene, John C., David Berry, Robert E. Coughlin, James Farnum, Eric Kelly, Thomas Plaut, and Ann Louise Strong. 1976. *Untaxing Open Space: An Evaluation of the Effectiveness of Differential Assessment on Farms and Open Space.* Washington, DC: Council on Environmental Quality.

Kovacs, Kent F. 2009. "The Timing of Rapid Farmland Conversion Events: Evidence from California's Differential Assessment Program." Paper presented at Agricultural and Applied Economics Associations 2009 Joint Annual Meeting, Milwaukee, July 26–28.

Ladd, Helen F. 1980. "The Considerations Underlying Preferential Tax Treatment of Open Space and Agricultural Land." In *Property Tax Preferences for Agricul-*

tural Land, ed. Neal A. Roberts and H. James Brown, chap. 2. Montclair, NJ: Allanheld, Osmun, & Co.

Lopez, Rigoberto A., Farhed A. Shah, and Marilyn A. Altobello. 1994. "Amenity Benefits and the Optimal Allocation of Land." *Land Economics* 70(1) (February):53–62.

Mark, Shelley M., Hiroshi Yamauchi, and Glenn M. Okimoto. 1982. "Differential Assessment and State Land Use Controls in Hawaii." *Annals of Regional Science* 16(3) (November):95–100.

Marshall, Alfred. 1948. *Principles of Economics*. 8th ed. New York: Macmillan.

Morris, Adele C. 1998. "Property Tax Treatment of Farmland: Does Tax Relief Delay Land Development?" In *Local Government Tax and Land Use Policies in the United States*, ed. Helen F. Ladd, 144–167. Cheltenham, UK: Edward Elgar.

Natural Resources Conservation Service. 2013. *2007 National Resources Inventory: Land Use Status and Trends*. Washington, DC: U.S. Department of Agriculture.

New Hampshire Department of Revenue Administration. 2010. *Current Use Report*. http://www.revenue.nh.gov/munc_prop/current_use/reports.htm.

Ohio Department of Taxation. 2010. "2010 Current Agricultural Use Value of Land Tables: Explanation of the Calculation of Values for Various Soil Mapping Units for Tax Year 2010." www.tax.ohio.gov/divisions/real_property/documents/CAUV _Memorandum_2010.pdf.

Ohio State University, Department of Agricultural, Environmental, and Development Economics. "OSU Farm Management: Farm Management Enterprise Budgets." http://aede.osu.edu/research/osu-farm-management/enterprise-budgets.

Park, Timothy, Mary Ahearn, Theodore Covey, Ken Erickson, Michael Harris, Jennifer Ifft, Christopher McGath, Mitch Morehart, Stephen Vogel, Jeremy G. Weber, and Robert Williams. 2011. *Agricultural Income and Finance Outlook, 2011 Edition*. USDA Economic Research Service. Outlook No. AIS-91.

Parks, Peter J., and Wilma Rose H. Quimio. 1996. "Preserving Agricultural Land with Farmland Assessment: New Jersey as a Case Study." *Agricultural and Resource Economics Review* 25(1) (April):22–27.

Polyakov, Maksym, and Daowei Zhang. 2008. "Property Tax Policy and Land-Use Change." *Land Economics* 84(3):396–408.

Purdue University Department of Agricultural Economics, Cooperative Extension Service. 2010. "Farm Land Assessment for Property Taxes." Indiana Local Government Information website. www.agecon.purdue.edu/crd/localgov/topics /essays/Prop_Tax_FarmLand_Asmt.htm.

Rodgers, Pamela H., and Gerry H. Williams. 1983. "A Survey of Use-Value Assessment Laws in the South." SRDC Series No. 53. Southern Rural Development Center, Mississippi State University.

Schwartz, S. I., D. E. Hansen, and T. C. Foin. 1975. "Preferential Taxation and the Control of Urban Sprawl: An Analysis of the California Land Conservation

Act." *Journal of Environmental Economics and Management* 2(2) (December):120–134.

Sexton, Terri A., Steven M. Sheffrin, and Arthur O'Sullivan. 1999. "Proposition 13: Unintended Effects and Feasible Reforms." *National Tax Journal* 52(1) (March):99–111.

Skouras, A. 1978. "The Non-Neutrality of Land Taxation." *Public Finance* 33(1–2): 113–134.

Tideman, T. Nicholas. 1982. "A Tax on Land Is Neutral." *National Tax Journal* 35: 109–111.

United Press. "Levitt to Build on Bel Air Farm." *New York Times*, August 28, 1957.

U.S. Department of Agriculture and President's Council on Environmental Quality. 1981. *Executive Summary of Final Report: National Agricultural Lands Study.* Washington, DC: U.S. Government Printing Office.

U.S. Department of Agriculture. 2007. *Census of Agriculture*, Vol. 1, Ch. 1: State Level Data.

Veseth, Michael. 1979. "Alternative Policies for Preserving Farm and Open Areas: Analysis and Evaluation of Available Options." *American Journal of Economics and Sociology* 38(1) (January):97–109.

Wisconsin Department of Revenue. 2010. *Agricultural Assessment Guide for Wisconsin Property Owners 2010.* www.revenue.wi.gov/pubs/slf/pb061.pdf.

———. 2012. *Wisconsin Property Assessment Manual 2012.* http://www.revenue.wi.gov/html/govpub.html.

Youngman, Joan M. 2005. "Taxing and Untaxing Land." *State Tax Notes* (September 5):727–738.

About the Authors

JOHN E. ANDERSON is the Baird Family Professor of Economics at the University of Nebraska–Lincoln and visiting fellow at the Lincoln Institute of Land Policy. Tax policy is the focus of his research and work. He has advised government agencies in the United States and around the world, including a turn from 2005 to 2006 with the President's Council of Economic Advisers in Washington, DC.

RICHARD W. ENGLAND is professor of economics at the University of New Hampshire–Durham and visiting fellow at the Lincoln Institute of Land Policy. His research and public speaking focus on property taxation, land development, conservation, and housing markets. Together with Richard F. Dye, he edited *Land Value Taxation: Theory, Evidence, and Practice* (2009).

Index

ACA. *See* Agricultural credit associations (ACA)

Accessibility, value of, 84, 85–86, 85(figure)

Agricultural credit associations (ACA), 118

Agricultural land: defined, 46, 47, 59, 62, 63, 65, 70, 73, 89–90, 112; protection of as national policy, 11. *See also* Development conversion; Land use change

Agricultural land price, agricultural land value and, 86–87

Agricultural land value, 84, 85, 85(figure), 86–87; defined, 58; economic impact of use-value assessment on, 95–96; improvements and, 90–91, 107–108; market value *vs.*, 86–88, 96, 141–142. *See also* Land values

Agricultural use value: calculating, 89–93; defined, 86–87

Agricultural zoning, 6, 90

Alabama use-value assessment program: assessment method, 31–32; development penalty/rollback penalties, 26(table), 32, 140; eligibility for, 31; eligible uses, 31; statutes, 31

Alaska use-value assessment program: assessment method, 32–33; commercial agricultural minimum, 24(table); development penalty/ rollback penalties, 26(table), 33; eligibility for, 24(table), 32; eligible uses, 32; recent use values, 33; statutes, 32

Allais, Maurice, 145n2

Application and renewal process, for use-value assessment programs, 28–31(table); recommendations for reform of, 147–148. *See also individual states*

Application for rezoning, use-value assessment eligibility and, 33, 136

Arizona, growth of developed land in, 5, 6(table)

Arizona use-value assessment program: application process, 28(table); assessment method, 33–34; development penalty, 34, 140; eligibility requirements, 33, 136–137; eligible uses, 33; land use change and, 23; statutes, 33

Arkansas use-value assessment program: assessment method, 34; development penalty, 34; eligible uses, 34; recent use values, 34; statutes, 34

Arrow, Kenneth, 145n2

Assessment method. *See* Income capitalization approach

Assessment ratio, 15n7, 81–82, 108

Averaging methods, 99, 103, 103(figure), 105, 105(table), 149

Bedford (New Hampshire), 3

Bid rents, 79–81, 80(figure)

Building value on agricultural land, 90–91, 107–108

California, growth of developed land in, 6(table)

California Land Conservation Act (CLCA), 16, 34

California use-value assessment program (Williamson Act), 16–17; assessment length, 35; contract length, 35, 141; conveyance penalties in, 27(table); development penalty, 35; eligibility

Eligibility for use-value assessment programs); enactment of, 14–21; enrollment in, 120–121, 135–138; example (Bedford, NH), 3–4; extensive margin and, 78; extent of use of, 6–7, 7(table); family farms and, 8, 12, 12n3, 13, 14–15, 121–123, 133; legal obstacles to enactment of, 15–16; market value assessments *vs.*, 7, 8(table), 13–14, 86–88, 96, 141–142; minimum acreage requirements, 22(table); negative consequences of, 8–9; overview, 82–84; penalty provisions, inadequacy of, 139–141. (*see also* Development penalties); preservation of rural landscape and, 123–127; principles for rational, 143–147; reasons for adoption of, 4–6, 11–14; recommended reforms of, 147–151; revenue-generating capacity of municipal government and, 6–7; shift in property tax burden and, 4, 8–9, 81–82, 94–95, 127–131, 133, 141–142; social cost of, 95, 96; state methods of use-value assessment estimation, 138–139; uniformity of taxation principle and, 8, 15–16. *See also individual states*

Use-value estimation methods, consistent with economic and financial principles, 148–150. *See also* Income capitalization approach

Use values, recent. *See individual states*

Utah use-value assessment program: assessment method, 68; development penalty/rollback penalties, 26(table), 68; eligibility requirements, 67–68; eligible uses, 67; recent use values, 68; statutes, 67

UVA. *See* Use-value assessment (UVA) programs

Vermont use-value assessment program: application process, 31(table); assessment method, 69; development penalty/conveyance penalties, 27, 27(table), 69, 140–141; eligibility

requirements, 68–69; eligible uses, 68; recent use values, 69; statutes, 68

Virginia (Fairfax County), use-value assessment application process in, 30(table)

Virginia use-value assessment program: assessment method, 70; case study, 112–117; development penalty/rollback penalties, 26(table), 70; eligibility requirements, 69–70; eligible uses, 69; statutes, 69

Washington use-value assessment program: application process, 31(table); assessment method, 71; development penalty/rollback penalties, 26(table), 71; eligibility requirements, 71; eligible uses, 71; shift of property tax burden and, 128–129; statutes, 70

West Virginia, uniformity of taxation principle, 16

West Virginia use-value assessment program: assessment method, 72; development penalty, 72; eligibility requirements, 72; eligible uses, 71; statutes, 71

Wetlands Reserve Program, 110

Whitman, Christie, 9

Williamson Act. *See* California use-value assessment program (Williamson Act)

Wisconsin use-value assessment program, 20–21; assessment method, 72–73; case study, 117–119; development penalty/rollback penalties, 26(table), 73; eligibility requirements, 72; eligible uses, 72; lack of zoning requirements for eligibility, 90; recent use values, 73; statutes, 20, 21, 72

Working waterfront land, 47

Wyoming use-value assessment program: assessment method, 73–74; eligibility requirements, 73; eligible uses, 73; recent use values, 74; statutes, 73

Zoning, agricultural, 6, 90

Zoning ordinances, 80n2

ABOUT THE
Lincoln Institute of Land Policy

The Lincoln Institute of Land Policy is a private operating foundation whose mission is to improve the quality of public debate and decisions in the areas of land policy and land-related taxation in the United States and around the world. The Institute's goals are to integrate theory and practice to better shape land policy and to provide a nonpartisan forum for discussion of the multidisciplinary forces that influence public policy. This focus on land derives from the Institute's founding objective—to address the links between land policy and social and economic progress—which was identified and analyzed by political economist and author Henry George.

The work of the Institute is organized in three departments: Valuation and Taxation, Planning and Urban Form, and International Studies, which includes programs on Latin America and China. We seek to inform decision making through education, research, policy evaluation, demonstration projects, and the dissemination of information through our publications, website, and other media. Our programs bring together scholars, practitioners, public officials, policy makers, journalists, and citizens in a collegial learning environment. The Institute does not take a particular point of view, but rather serves as a catalyst to facilitate analysis and discussion of land use and taxation issues—to make a difference today and to help policy makers plan for tomorrow. The Lincoln Institute of Land Policy is an equal opportunity institution.

LINCOLN INSTITUTE
OF LAND POLICY

113 Brattle Street
Cambridge, MA 02138-3400 USA

Phone: 1-617-661-3016 or 1-800-526-3873
Fax: 1-617-661-7235 or 1-800-526-3944
E-mail: help@lincolninst.edu
Web: www.lincolninst.edu